TRUTHS THAT SET US FREE

Bestselling author of THE POWER OF YOUR SUBCONSCIOUS MIND

DR. JOSEPH MURPHY

FP CLASSICS

Published 2024

FINGERPRINT! CLASSICS

Prakash Books

Fingerprint Publishing
@FingerprintP
@fingerprintpublishingbooks
www.fingerprintpublishing.com

The author of this book does not dispense medical advice or prescribe the use of any technique as a form of treatment for physical, emotional, or medical problems without the advice of a physician, either directly or indirectly. The intent of the author is only to offer information of a general nature to help you in your quest for emotional and spiritual well-being. In the event you use any of the information in this book for yourself, which is your constitutional right, the author and the publisher assume no responsibility for your actions.

ISBN: 978 93 8905 380 7

CONTENTS

1

Great Bible Truths for Human Problems

> *And he said unto them, What man shall there be among you, that shall have one sheep, and if it fall into a pit on the Sabbath day, will he not lay hold on it, and lift it out? How much then is a man better than a sheep? Wherefore it is lawful to do well on the Sabbath days. Then saith he to the man, Stretch forth thine hand. And he stretched it forth; and it was restored whole, like as the other* (Matthew 12:11-13).

The twelfth chapter of Matthew is a wonderful exposition on mental and spiritual healing. Jesus was at that state of consciousness where he could heal instantly, so the man stretched forth his hand.

There is also an inner meaning to stretching forth the hand. For example, the man with an inferiority or rejection complex is not using the Infinite Power and Wisdom within him. He fails to see that the Presence of God—the Almighty Power—is within his own subjective depths, enabling him to do wonderful things.

How a Salesman Stretched Forth His Hand

A salesman who attended my lectures and special classes in Los Angeles from time to time was not making ends meet, was down on himself and felt inferior to all the other salesmen in his company. At my suggestion, he began to affirm: "I am a son of the Living God, and I am expressing more and more of God's light, love, truth and beauty. I am a tremendous success in all my endeavors and my sales are improving every day in a wonderful way. Every time I visit a customer I affirm silently, 'The Spirit (God) in me salutes the Spirit (God) in you. It is God talking to God, and the result is harmony, peace, Divine understanding and right action between us.'"

This was his prayer night and morning. He affirmed and reiterated these truths three or four times out loud night and morning, knowing that these meaningful truths would sink into his subconscious and activate the latent powers within him. He learned and understood that his subconscious mind would accept what he sincerely believed in his conscious mind. The subconscious accepts your convictions and what you predominantly think and believe.

In a month's time his whole life became changed. He established wonderful relations with his customers, sales improved and he no longer felt inferior. He continued to contemplate himself as a son of the Infinite, while at the same time recognizing the Divinity in everybody else. He stretched forth his hand and manifested the Power of the Infinite within him. His constant affirmation is: "I can do all things through the God-Power which strengtheneth me."

How to Use the Healing Power for Yourself or Another

The Infinite Healing Presence indwells all men and women. Everyone has the gift of healing, for God is the reality of everyone. This is how you can pray for healing for a loved one or a friend: Feel the Presence of God, which is the Presence of vitality, wholeness, power, intelligence, peace and harmony, permeating his whole being, functioning in him and through him. Realize that he or she is being Divinely watched over. The other person may not know about it. You accept what you affirmed and believe it.

Praying for another is thinking of the qualities and attributes of God. Get interested, not tense, e.g., if you are on a train, bus or subway and you see a sign and read the subject matter, you become very interested. Likewise, become very interested in the Divine Healing Presence, and as you rise in consciousness, you will have power.

You can affirm that he or she is being healed now. Feel the Presence of God there and realize that he or she is now externalizing the vitality, wholeness, power and intelligence, which Pure Spirit is. Believe it, accept it, then leave it. If you think of the person later on, do it again, as if you had never prayed before for that person. If it is someone close to you, do it several times a day.

The healing may come slowly or quickly, according to your faith or belief. That is called in the Bible "sending your word, your thought and your feeling to the other." The person for whom you are praying receives your affirmation. The result is that the sick person's subconscious mind becomes thoroughly imbued with the realization of its own healing power; and according to the laws of the subconscious mind, the latter brings forth into external manifestation that which is impressed upon it. Thus, health is substituted for sickness.

Remember, however, when you pray for another you must never be in a critical mood or a tense state of mind, for you can't storm the gates . . . *In quietness and in confidence shall be your strength* . . . (Isaiah 30:15).

How a Mother Prayed for the So-Called Dull Son

A teacher said to a mother: "I think your son is somewhat retarded.

He is dull; he seems hopeless and cannot learn or be taught." The mother loved the boy, though, and prayed for him in this way: "I claim, feel, know and believe that the Infinite Intelligence of the Infinite One is welling up within him. I know that the wisdom of God is working out through him, and that his intellect is anointed with the light and love of the Infinite. My boy is a perfect expression of the Infinite Healing Presence."

She affirmed these truths for about ten minutes every morning, afternoon and night, knowing that she would resurrect the qualities and attributes of God lodged in the subjective depths of the boy. Following the contemplation of these truths, she made it a special point to imagine that her son was right in front of her, telling her: "Mother, look at my report card. The teacher praised me." She heard this over and over again in a relaxed and passive state of mind, knowing that her mental image must agree with her affirmation.

The mental image you have is always made manifest. The boy gradually became more responsive, and he excelled in his studies. He confirmed objectively what she affirmed and imaged subjectively.

For by thy words thou shalt be justified, and by thy words thou shalt be condemned (Matthew 12:37). To justify is to make equal, to balance the imbalance. Her realization of the truth about her boy was resurrected in the mind of her son, which balanced the equation. The 'word' in the Bible is your thought-feeling, your conviction, your dominant belief, is always made manifest.

How to Gain More Faith

You do everything by faith. You plant seeds in the ground because you have faith in the laws of agriculture. You bake a cake by faith and you drive your car by faith. Everyone has faith. Some, unfortunately, have faith in failure, in sickness, in lack and in limitation. This is faith in the wrong thing. Have faith in success, achievement, health, happiness and abundance. Have faith in the creative law of your mind, and as you apply the law of your mind constructively, you will grow in faith. Have faith in Divine guidance, Divine right action, the abundance of the Infinite and the goodness of God in the land of the living.

How to Develop Faith in God and Forgiveness

There is a price to be paid, but all men and women can pay that price by giving up feeling sorry for themselves, ceasing all self-condemnation and self-criticism and condemnation of others, and entering into the spirit of forgiveness of themselves and others. When the thought of resentment of another comes to your mind, affirm: "I release you and wish for you all the blessings of life." As you continue to do that, the person will come to your mind and there will be no sting. In other words, you will no longer mentally sizzle—then you will know you have forgiven and forgotten.

Watch the Idle Words

But I say unto you, That every idle word that men shall speak, they shall give account thereof in the day of judgment (Matthew 12:36). The negative thoughts, the doubts and fears, are the idle words which prevent healing or advancement.

Every day and hour is the day of judgment. When you pray for another, that is your judgment, the decision you arrived at. You realized the Presence of God, i.e., health, vitality and wholeness; or you dwelt on the sickness in him. How did you judge him? If you saw a diseased man and hoped he would be better, you judged wrongly. If you saw a perfectly healthy man (in other words, if you visioned him as he ought to be—vital, strong and bubbling over with enthusiasm and energy), you judged correctly.

When Will the Answer to My Prayer Come to Pass?

But of that day and that hour knoweth no man, no, not the angels which are in heaven, neither the Son, but the Father (Mark 13:32). *Watch ye therefore: for ye know not when the master of the house cometh, at even, or at midnight, or at the cockcrowing, or in the morning* (Mark 13:35).

All seeds mature and germinate at different periods according to their kind; likewise, seeds or impressions made in your subconscious mind mature and come to full bloom at different periods—days, months, sometimes years. Your desire or idea, when impregnated in your subconscious, gestates in the darkness; and the wisdom of your subconscious determines when to present the answer or manifestation full-blown into your experience.

The Reason the Old Ailment Returns

During consultation, a man said that he had been completely healed of ulcers but that later the condition had returned. I gathered in talking with him that some years ago he had been in business and his partner had embezzled funds and had absconded to Canada. Recently he heard that his ex-partner was very successful in business and also had become quite wealthy. This made him very agitated and resentful.

He was living the role over again and reinfecting himself. The memory was not withered, not forgotten and not forgiven. The roots of resentment and hostility were still lurking in the recesses of his subconscious and, like a festering wound, sending psychic pus throughout his system. His ulcerated thoughts and emotions reactivated his ulcers.

I explained to him that forgiveness of himself and the other was absolutely essential for his health and well being and that he would know when he had forgiven because he could remember the incident and remain indifferent altogether—no feeling, no word. By living the scene or experience over again, he recreated the condition, and like the seed that recedes and grows again quarterly, annually, or biennially in the same way, the old ulcerated state appeared in a new form. Certain plants die and bud again according to season. It is essential to eradicate the cause to prevent a relapse of the disease. He decided definitely to release him completely in his mind, wishing for his ex-partner all the blessings of life, and a healing followed.

The Proof that You Are Free from Bitterness and Hostility

Can you see the other person as happy, harmonious, joyous, etc.? If not, you have not forgiven or forsaken. These are the weeds you must pluck out. The roots are still there, and the roots of bitterness wither by indifference. This is another way to kill that root: Listen to the voice of the other person who wronged you telling you what a wonderful, dignified person you are and how honest and kind you are. Make it real. You want to hear it. Get into the mood of that mental picture. It works.

How Often Should I Pray about a Problem?

I am often asked that question. You can't make a universal rule for prayer-therapy or scientific prayer. The particular person has to be considered, together with the way he looks at the problem or difficulty. You can pray in different ways at different times. For example, you might use the 91st Psalm in the morning, the 23rd Psalm at noon and the 27th Psalm at night.

If you are praying for your mother for peace and harmony and a healing, the best way would be to mention your mother's name and contemplate peace, harmony, wholeness, beauty and the vitality and life of the Infinite flowing through her making her whole and perfect. You should also claim that Infinite Intelligence is guiding the doctors and nurses and all who minister to her. Surround her and all who are helping her with light, love, truth and beauty. Continue praying along these lines until you feel relaxed and satisfied.

Decree that your prayer is working now. Don't say, "This prayer will do now. I will pray again in a couple of hours." This attitude neutralizes your prayer. Know that your prayer is effective now, and pray later on when you have gotten away from the previous prayer session. This means that in a normal day you are busy about other things—your business, home, profession, etc. In other words, you will have forgotten about it for several hours. Then you can begin prayer-therapy for your mother once again, and continue in like manner until she is well and happy. Each time you pray you are reinforcing the idea of wholeness and perfect health in your subconscious, which will be resurrected in your mother's mind and body.

Be sure to avoid picking and nagging at the problem from time to time. Relax and believe, and wonders will happen as you pray. Realize it is the Infinite Presence thinking and healing through you.

How His Acne Disappeared

A young boy of eighteen said he had been using lotions, ointments and getting injections. His acne would temporarily disappear and then periodically recur. The doctor called his condition an inflammatory disease of the sebaceous glands, characterized by postural eruptions on his face.

The real trouble, however, was that he was frustrated. He wanted to be an aviator, but his father objected and said he should learn the business of his father and succeed him when he would retire. There was warfare in his mind. His skin, being an organ of elimination and symbolic of an envelope of Divine love, revealed the hidden conflict.

He faced the problem and discussed the matter with his father. The latter saw the cause of the trouble and thereupon released his son, letting him become what he desired. The pustules disappeared within a week.

How Her Prayer Was Answered by Contemplating the Happy Ending

While lecturing at the Unity Temple in New Orleans a few years ago, I had a consultation with a woman who desired to have a child, but her gynecologist said she had tumors in the womb and advised strongly against it. She had wanted a child for over six years.

This woman was a profound student of the healing techniques of the Bible. She was particularly interested in the following verses: *And it shall come to pass, while my glory passeth by, that I will put thee in a cliff of the rock, and will cover thee with my hand while I pass by: And I will take away mine hand, and thou shall see my back parts: but my face shall not be seen* (Exodus 33:22-23).

The application of the truths of these verses solved her problem. God, or Living Spirit Almighty, or Consciousness, has no back parts, as your Awareness or I AMness is invisible, but you do see the manifestation of your faith or conviction in God. When the sun has set the day is over. I see the back parts of it—the setting sun. Face is the secret. There is no form, figure or face to your deep-seated conviction or belief. The rock means your conviction.

I explained to her that as she turned to the Infinite Healing Presence which created her, knowingly and believingly, she was standing on a rock; that her faith or confidence had become fixed in the belief of giving birth to a child in Divine order; and that God would cover her with His hand, meaning the Overshadowing Presence would give her rest and peace, the protection for her new mental attitude. When the hand (the Power and Presence of God) is removed, you see the back parts—the manifestation of the desire. If I am coming toward you, you see my face; but if I walk past you, you only see my back. The Infinite Presence has no back parts, it's simply the objectification of your desire.

Accordingly, she prayed as follows: "God's Healing Love is flowing through me, permeating my whole being. I AM relaxed and at ease, knowing that the Infinite Healing Presence brings this to pass in its own way and in Divine order. I let go and let God take over. With my imaginary hands, I am fondling, cosseting and cuddling my baby in my arms."

She affirmed these truths night and morning, feelingly and meaningfully, knowing that by repetition, faith and expectancy, these truths would sink into her subconscious and come to pass. Shortly afterwards, she did become pregnant and in the ninth month gave birth to a boy who was perfect in all ways. The obstetrician found no tumors. They had been dissolved by her constant spiritual transfusions. She saw the back parts, Biblically speaking, i.e., the manifestation, the happy ending, the objectification of her desire. There was no tension, no anxiety: just a quiet assurance that the Healing Presence was flowing through her and would bring things to pass in its own way and in Divine order. When you pray, imagine the happy ending, the Divine solution, through the wisdom of the Infinite. Relax and believe, and when you relax, let go and believe, you experience the joy of the answered prayer.

Do Not Deny What You Affirm

When you want a healing of any condition, get silent, relax, think of the Infinite Presence and Power, and affirm that the healing is taking place now. There must be no resentment or bitterness. Forgive everyone. Your subconscious made your body and it can restore you to the Pattern on the Mount. If you can't heal yourself, go to a doctor and bless him and pray for him. To think because you go to a doctor you should not pray is rank superstition.

When you think of the condition from time to time, affirm immediately: "God is healing me now." To fret and fuss and deny and say, "I'm getting worse," "Prayer doesn't work," "I'm hopeless," or "I'm doing something wrong" is somewhat as if a surgeon operated on you, cut out the appendix, and then in ten minutes ran back and opened you up again to see how you were getting along or to see if he had forgotten something, and then in a half an hour again ran back and sewed you up again. He would probably kill you by blood poisoning or shock. You will have to account for every idle word you speak, for the simple reason that your subconscious mind takes you literally and brings all your beliefs to pass.

How a Father Healed His Son

While speaking some time ago in Pawtucket, Rhode Island, a man consulted with me about his son. He was divorced, and he said his former wife had poisoned the mind of his son against him so that when he went to visit the boy, he would run out the back door and disappear into a neighbor's home. He went through the courts trying to get custody of the boy but failed. He offered his ex-wife considerable money over and above the legal settlement in order to get custody of the boy, but she refused. The boy was not getting on well in school and was hateful towards his father, as he had been taught that he didn't want him.

I suggested that he try the spiritual approach to the problem, since the human approach had failed. He prayed as follows: "I surrender my ex-wife to the Infinite Presence and Power. She is Divinely led in all ways, and Divine love fills her soul. God flows through her, filling up all the empty vessels in her life." Whenever he thought of her, he would immediately affirm, "I released you. God loves you and cares for you."

He also prayed for his son: "Bill, my son, is in his true place, ministered to by Divine love, harmony, peace and understanding. He knows the truth, he loves the truth, and he hears the truth. There are peace, harmony, love and understanding between us." Whenever he thought of Bill, he would affirm, "Divine love watches over Bill."

I received a letter some time later from this man telling me that his ex-wife had called him up saying Bill was sick. He went over and had a wonderful reunion with his son. She wanted him to take the boy, as she had fallen in love with another man and was delighted to release Bill to his father. This was a perfect working of the Law . . . *What things soever ye desire, when ye pray, believe that ye receive them, and ye shall have them* (Mark 11:24).

Your Inner Conviction Is Always Made Manifest

You do not pretend to be vital, strong and healthy when you are sick. Admit your sickness. Realize that nothing is forever and that you can and will overcome the condition through your knowledge of mental and spiritual laws. It is foolish to pretend you are getting better when obviously you are getting worse. There is no use trying to mesmerize yourself by calling black "white."

You turn away from the problem and contemplate the Healing Power of God and His guidance; and as you cleave to that positive Truth, conditions will improve. When the outer condition improves, you are on the right track. Remember that if, after prayer-therapy, the outer picture does not change in a reasonable time (hours or days), you are deceiving yourself. You are not working correctly. When the outer condition is changing, you are getting results.

Remember, your mental attitude, your real inner conviction, is always made manifest. Cease all excuses and prevarications of any kind, because when you pray, health springs forth speedily. Lessening of the pain and disappearance of the condition tells the story. This is the Truth which sets you free. *Wherefore by their fruits ye shall know them* (Matthew 7:20).

2

The Bible's Formula for Victory—the Horse and the Rider

And Moses stretched out his hand over the sea; and the Lord caused the sea to go back by a strong east wind all that night, and made the sea dry land, and the waters were divided. And the children of Israel went into the midst of the sea upon the dry ground: and the waters were a wall unto them on their right hand, and on their left. And the Egyptians pursued, and went in after them to the midst of the sea, even all Pharaoh's horses, his chariots, and his horsemen (Exodus 14:21-23).

Scientific prayer consists in really knowing that before you call, the answer is there and waiting for you to receive it . . . *Before they call I will answer; and while they are yet speaking, I will hear* (Isaiah 65:24).

"All things be ready if the mind be so" (Shakespeare).

The Power that Answers Prayer

It is well to remember that every man answers his own prayer, because his subconscious responds to his conviction . . . *If thou canst believe, all things are possible to him that believeth* (Mark 9:23).

Do not look to a king on a throne, who must be cajoled into an act of grace. Rather, the answer is based on your complete acceptance of the wish fulfilled. Most people look to others for favors, security and promotion. This is a mistake and is due to lack of understanding. Why look to another? God is all there is and the Source of all things, visible and invisible.

. . . *God, who giveth us richly all things to enjoy* (I Timothy 6:17). *But my God shall supply all your need according to his riches in glory* . . . (Philippians 4:19).

This Presence and Power is in all, over all and through all. It is Omnipresent and, therefore, is within you. The contact is made within through your thought and feeling, which are Divine agencies, referred to as the Father within you. Your thought and feeling father or create your destiny and all your experiences, conditions and circumstances. You can't be outside that which is all in all.

The One and Only Power

The Bible calls this Power, I AM, which means Being, life, awareness, unconditioned consciousness, Self-Originating Spirit. All things are made by the self-contemplation of Spirit, or God. It creates by Itself, becoming the thing It creates.

. . . *Before Abraham was, I AM* (John 8:58). This means before any objectification or manifestation of ideals or desires takes place, the unconditioned or formless awareness (I AM) conditions Itself into the image and likeness of your concept or ideal.

The Right Approach to Prayer

Your approach to prayer must always be: *Call unto me, and I will answer thee, and shew thee great and mighty things, which thou knowest not* (Jeremiah 33:3).

Never use the term, "if it's right for me." This shows a complete lack of understanding of the laws of your mind and the way of the Infinite Spirit within you. There is no if in prayer. This implies doubt and confusion, and this attitude of mind manifests its likeness in our world, which results in a confused, chaotic state of affairs.

In the 21st through 23rd verses of Exodus set forth in the beginning of this chapter, you are told exactly how to pray and overcome any condition. Moses means any man who draws forth from his subjective depths faith and confidence in the great truth that . . . *With God all things are possible* (Matthew 19:26) and . . . *If thou canst believe, all things are possible to him that believeth* (Mark 9:23).

The Bible uses historical characters metaphorically. Moses means drawing out from the water. In other words, you draw out from your subjective depths inspiration, illumination, intuition, strength and wisdom, enabling you to do the so-called impossible. It is your mental attitude that prevails and governs your experience. Changed attitudes change everything in your life.

Stretching out the hand, as mentioned in Verse 21, is expanding your awareness of the Power of God within you, making for a sense of oneness with the Infinite. With the hand you fashion, mold, create, shape and direct. This represents the creative power of God.

The sea means the disturbed, turbulent, emotional state of mind. This state subsides when you tune in with the Infinite and experience the river of peace and love flowing through you, exhilarating and vitalizing your whole being. This is called dividing the waters, or separating the chaff from the wheat, the false from the truth. The mood of confidence and peace, knowing that the action of God is taking place, causes the negative fears, doubts and emotional turmoil to vanish even as the sun dissipates the mist.

The east wind mentioned in Verse 21 is symbolic of the birth of God in your mind. The sun rises in the east to open and govern the day. Symbolically speaking, it means the resurrection or birth of God in your mind and the wonders that will happen to you because of this discovery and awareness. The east wind is, therefore, symbolic of the victorious spirit of man who has enthroned the God-like concept of triumph in his mind.

Let the East Wind Move You Now

When the east wind moves in us, it is the Spirit of God animating us and causing us to move onward, upward and God-ward. The children of Israel that move forward on dry land are our ideas, dreams and aspirations, which become subjectified by feeling the reality of them; then they are projected on the screen of space (dry land).

In Verse 23 it says the Egyptians pursued them. Egypt in the Bible stands for fear, doubt and limitation of all kinds, the belief that externals control you. The Egyptians hated a shepherd, one who thinks God-like thoughts. This means if you are a good shepherd, the "Egyptians" hate you because your spiritual thoughts are going to annihilate and conquer the negative thoughts.

Oftentimes, when you are praying and trusting in the Omnipotence of God, negative thoughts will come into your mind, saying to you, "You can't do that," "You don't have the power," "It's impossible," etc. Look how formidable these negative thoughts are. When you are praying for a loved one, you find the verdict of the doctor, or nurse, or well-meaning neighbor trying to dissuade you from your conviction of the miraculous healing power of the Infinite Presence within you. This is the challenge, or fight, that goes on in your own mind.

When you know the law of mind you are a relaxed player because you know in your innermost soul that Truth will win. *And all things, whatsoever ye shall ask in prayer, believing, ye shall receive* (Matthew 21:22). The scientific thinker knows that error must fail, since it has no power but the false beliefs and opinions of man. The sustained consciousness of peace and victory must prevail over all negative challenges. The song of Moses is the song of triumph and victory based on our subjective conviction, which anoints our intellect with wisdom and becomes a light upon our path, revealing to us the perfect plan and showing us the way we should go.

For Thine Is the Power

. . . *There is no power but of God: the powers that be are ordained of God* (Romans 13:1). Persistently affirm that there is no power but that released by God, the Living Spirit Almighty within you. It will be a usable and powerful truth when you once get it fixed in your mind, an ever present help, a comforter and a protector. *Thou shalt have no other gods before me* (Exodus 20:3).

The God that millions all over the world beg and beseech is the Deep Self of you, the Divine Presence within you. Many religious dogmatists frighten people into thinking that God is some tyrannical being living somewhere in the heavens—a God of vengeance, a mysterious stranger. A poet referred to God: "Closer is He than breathing; nearer than hands and feet."

From an absolute point of view, God cannot be known, for nothing can be known in the absolute sense of the term. But there is much we can learn, such as that thoughts are things; what we feel we attract and what we imagine we become. Our thoughts are creative, and whatever we impress on our subconscious is expressed. We can keep on tapping the infinite reservoirs of wisdom and power within us, since there is no end to the powers and intelligence of the Infinite within us. Job says: *He . . . hangeth the earth upon nothing* (Job 26:7).

The only creative power you know is your thought. There can be only one Creative Power—this is true mathematically, scientifically and spiritually. If there were two powers, one would cancel out the other and there would be chaos everywhere. Science knows we live in a mathematically ordered universe. This is why there is a state of order, design, and purpose in the universe. There could not possibly be two Infinites. Infinity is without beginning or end. The Bible gives the answer: *Hear, O Israel: the Lord our God is one Lord* (Deuteronomy 6:4).

The Red Sea that all of us go through represents the challenges, difficulties, problems, illnesses and vexations we overcome as we call on the Infinite Presence and Power, which responds to us as harmony, peace, love and the joy of the answered prayer. We cross the Red Sea of fear, dogma, traditions, ignorance, fear and superstition and discover the joy of the Lord, which is our strength.

And I will bring the blind by a way that they knew not; I will lead them in paths that they have not known: I will make darkness light before them, and crooked things straight. These things will I do unto them, and not forsake them (Isaiah 42:16).

The blind in the Bible are those who do not know that God indwells them, that He walks and talks in them, and is the very Life Principle within them.

The Father Within

When man awakens to the Light, he discovers his own consciousness (Awareness, Spirit) is the Father spoken of and the Creator of all experiences, circumstances and all things. It is called The Nameless One within and also The Formless One until we give It a name or form. The inventor has an idea in his mind. He gives it form by accepting it in his mind, and then he gives it form by clothing the idea or thought-image in form so men and women can use it. He gave form and expression to that which always subsisted in the mind of the Infinite.

Likewise, God becomes man by imagining and believing Himself to be man. The Formless and Nameless One now appears in the form of man. God limits Himself by becoming man. God created a being out of Himself, capable of returning joy to Himself. Man is here to Glorify God and enjoy Him forever.

The Horse and the Rider

. . . Sing ye to the Lord, for he hath triumphed gloriously; the horse and his rider hath he thrown into the sea (Exodus 15:21). Oftentimes you have seen horses and their riders on the bridle paths, climbing mountain

trails and moving along the roads of the country. You also see them running at the race track, and the jockeys seem to be perfect riders. The horses take the riders where they want to go. The horse instinctively knows that a master rides him because the master rider shows no fear. He loves his horse and he is in complete control.

Likewise, we must love the Infinite by giving this Presence within us all our allegiance, devotion and loyalty, recognizing It as the Only Power. That is called loving God, and as we practice this love of the Infinite, we can overcome, override and master any problem or situation that may confront us.

How Can I Love God?

Some say: How can I love an Infinite Spirit or Power? It is so vague and impersonal. How can I love a man or woman whom I don't know in this life? Love in the Bible is loyalty; it is putting God first in your life, while realizing that It is the Only Presence and Power. Love of God means to initiate a healthy, reverent, wholesome respect for the Divinity which created you, sustains you, and which gave you the whole world.

When you absolutely and positively refuse to give power to any created thing or to any person, place, condition or circumstance, then you are loving God. The scientific thinker does not give power to the phenomenalistic world; he gives all glory and power to the Infinite. He places the Creator above His creation. Also, you must remember that God and good are synonymous. When you give attention and devotion to honesty, integrity, peace, harmony, forbearance, goodwill and justice to all, you are also loving God, or good. As you practice radiating love and goodwill to all, this attitude of cordiality, geniality and good feeling insures success and happiness.

The Horsemen and Chariots of Pharaoh

And the waters returned, and covered the chariots, and the horsemen, and all the host of Pharaoh that came into the sea after them; there remained not so much as one of them (Exodus 14:28).

Pharaoh in the Bible means the five-sense natural man, governed by the five senses, worldly power and fear. The horsemen and chariots, which represent thoughts and emotions of fear, resentment, hate and greed, are drowned, dissipated and wiped out by the contemplation of the Presence of God. By filling your mind with eternal verities, you neutralize and expunge all fear and negative thoughts that are in the subconscious mind, and their embodiment must disappear also.

The horse and the rider, as mentioned in Exodus, represent the negative and destructive emotions of revenge, jealousy, hate and injustice, called the four vices. These should be replaced by the four virtues, which are love, justice, peace and integrity. Four (4) is symbolic of the four-footed animal or emotions of man. The tiger is in man. The sting of the wasp is also within him. The fox, or the sly, cunning states, are also in man. The dove of peace is within him also. As a matter of fact, all animals or animated states of consciousness are within man.

If you stop and think, you will realize that all moods and emotions are within you. Man's negative emotions, such as suppressed rage, resentment and hostility, surge up from his subliminal depths like the waves of the sea, carrying all manner of debris with them and casting them on the shores. Man must remember that his dominant feeling or emotion controls him, and he must ask himself if he is resentful or hateful. If so, he is riding for a big fall which may result in a worldly sense in some loathsome disease, accident, or some other discordant state.

If man's dominant emotion is resentment; he has established a tyrant in his mind and he will find that under the dominance of such an emotion, everything he does will be wrong. Negative emotions sap man's enthusiasm, vitality, hope, ambition and aspirations. When he wants to succeed in life, he fails. In fact, he finds himself going backward. The horse (negative emotions of hostility and resentment) carries him where it wants to go, and he has lost control and is thrown, just as a wild horse casts him off its back onto the ground.

Making Right Decisions

Remember the great truth: . . . *In quietness and in confidence shall be your strength* . . . (Isaiah 30:15). If you are disturbed, you cannot make right decisions, as your dominant emotion prevails. When you are disturbed, forgive yourself for harboring negative thoughts of any kind and follow these instructions: "I forgive myself for harboring negative thoughts, and I resolve not to engage in them any more. I also release all those whom I resent, wishing for them all the blessings of life. I know that when God's love fills my soul and His river of peace flows through, I cannot resent or hate the meanest man who walks the earth. I loose them all and I let them go. I know when I have forgiven everyone, for I can meet them in my mind and there is no longer any sting there. I am at peace."

When your mind is at peace, you can then ask for Divine guidance and direction, and the still, small voice will speak to you. It's a vibration; you will feel it. It is the inner silent knowing of the soul.

Longfellow revealed the vital nature of intuition, or being taught from within, when he wrote the following: "Let us, then, labor for an inner stillness, an inward stillness and an inward healing; that perfect silence where the lips and heart are still, and we no longer entertain our own imperfect thoughts and vain opinions, but God alone speaks in us, and we wait in singleness of heart that we may know His will, and in the silence of our spirits, that we may do His will, and do that only."

In other words, God speaks in the universal language of love, peace, inspiration and illumination. Paul says: *For God is not the author of confusion, but of peace* . . . (I Corinthians 14:33).

The Trained Rider

The horse knows the disciplined rider who masters his horse and who can lead him where he will, and if, perchance, he is thrown off the horse, he gets on again, pats the animal gently and rides off. He does not spend one moment in regret or in criticizing himself by self-accusation, such as, "Why did I fall off?" "I must be losing my grip," etc. No. The trained rider is too wise for that. Furthermore, he knows the horse would pick up his negative emotion and he would no longer be the master of the horse.

Your Real Master

Psychologically speaking, your dominant conviction about yourself is the real master of your thoughts, images, emotions, actions and reactions. Your dominant thought (or, you can call it your master thought) controls all the lesser thoughts and ideas in your mind. Ask yourself: Who is my boss? Let not fear be your dominant thought. If this is already so, you have instilled in your mind a destructive boss over your household. The true Lord should be a God of love enthroned in your mind, called the Lord God, or the law of goodness, truth and beauty.

What wonders would happen in your life if every morning before you went to work you got quiet, relaxed and turned within, affirming knowingly and feelingly: "God, the Life Principle in me, the Living Spirit, the Reality of me, is my guide and counselor today and every day. This Living Spirit in me is my way-shower, my boss, my adjuster, my paymaster, the Source of my supply, and I AM inspired and illumined from On High. Today and every day from now on, God thinks, speaks, acts and reacts through me and my words are words of wisdom, truth and beauty."

As you quietly, lovingly and meaningfully affirm the above truths, gradually they will become subjectified and your subconscious will compel you to experience these wonderful

This is the action of God. Sustain this mood and you will experience the Song of Moses, which is the joy of the answered prayer.

I will lift up mine eyes unto the hills, from whence cometh my help (Psalm 121:1).

3

Truths to Live By

> *For there is nothing covered, that shall not be revealed; neither hid, that shall not be known. Therefore whatsoever ye have spoken in darkness shall be heard in the light; and that which ye have spoken in the ear in closets shall be proclaimed upon the housetops* (Luke 12:2-3).

This means that whatever we decree meaningfully in the depths of our own mind will be made manifest for all to see. Many people seem to think that these paragraphs refer to the sins of the other fellow which will be exposed or revealed; e.g., the last day of judgment when all our sins would be placed on our forehead. However, people would not read them anyway, as they would be too busy with their own.

These verses refer to the laws of involution and evolution. In other words, whatever is involved in your mentality will be evolved or objectified in all phases of your life. It means the law of action and reaction. Fear, anger, love, joy and sadness will all be made manifest on the screen of space.

One man said to me, "I suffer here, and when I die I go to Paradise." All suffering is due to ignorance. I explained to him that Spirit, or God, couldn't suffer. We suffer because of our misuse and misapplication of the laws of mind. We suffer until we learn the laws of mind and the way of the Spirit. All the suffering and misery in the world is primarily due to ignorance. Ignorance then is the only sin, and all suffering is the consequence of it.

Why He Passed Away in a Bathtub

While attending a funeral recently, the surviving widow said to me that her husband had held a constant fear of drowning, which apparently went back to his childhood. He never went on a boat or near the ocean for fear of drowning, but she said he had died in the bathtub. This impression was made in his subconscious, and it fulfilled itself in its own way. He could have neutralized it at any time, but he rejected scientific prayer and refused to consult with anyone regarding that hidden fear.

This is why the Bible says there is nothing covered that shall not be revealed, which simply means that whatever is impressed in our subconscious mind will be made manifest on the screen of space and come forth as form, function, experience and events.

Having Done All, Stand

While speaking recently at the International New Thought Convention in Chicago, I had a long conversation with a medical doctor, who told me that many years ago he had tried every conceivable way to get into Yale Medical College and had pulled all the strings, but had failed. He tried other medical schools, with the same result.

His mother quoted some words from the Bible . . . *Having done all, to stand* (Ephesians 6:13). She said to him, "That means to stop running in circles; relax, let go, and stop trying with your conscious mind." She said, "You have done your best. Turn your request over to your subconscious mind and let the creative intelligence of your deeper mind solve it."

This was wise advice. The Second World War began about that time. He was drafted and, since he had the proper preliminary education, the Army sent him to medical college. His prayer was answered—not the way he expected, though, for the ways of the subconscious are past finding out. Therefore, whatsoever ye truths, for the nature of your subconscious is compulsive. Millions have forgotten the Lord God Jehovah, which means the state of consciousness which would bless, heal and inspire others.

Thus the Lord saved Israel that day out of the hand of the Egyptians; and Israel saw the Egyptians dead upon the sea shore (Exodus 14:30). Israel means a prince ruling with God; that is to say, anyone who believes in the sovereignty of the Spirit within and who is loyal to the One Power while recognizing no other power but the One is called Israel. Israel is saved from the Egyptians, which means the man who knows the law and prays scientifically by contemplating the truths of God from the highest standpoint, neutralizes and destroys all the negative thoughts which, in Biblical language, are described as Egyptians appearing dead upon the shore.

When you give your attention to the Almighty Power within you and contemplate the Divine solution to your problem or difficulty, attention being the key to life, all limited states fall away and die within us. We die to the old and we live to the new.

Then sang Moses and the children of Israel this song unto the Lord, and spake, saying, I will sing unto the Lord, for he hath triumphed gloriously: the horse and his rider hath he thrown into the sea (Exodus 15:1). This means the song of triumph in your soul, your conviction of joy and peace, while knowing that this attitude of mind divides the seas or turbulent states, and that the horse and the rider (the negative emotions) hath he thrown into the sea. In other words, the destructive emotion is transformed in the sea of your subconscious.

You can overcome any difficulty, whatever it may be, if you will become still and ask yourself quietly: "How is it in God and heaven?" The answer will steal over the arid areas of your mind like the dew of heaven, and the silent, inner knowing comes to you: "All is bliss, harmony, peace, joy, abundance, infinite intelligence, boundless wisdom, boundless love and indescribable beauty." All these are qualities of God submerged in your subconscious depths.

Whatever your prayer is, realize that God gave you the desire; feel the reality of it now, knowing you possess it already in your mind. As you do this, the Spirit of God will move on your behalf.

have spoken in darkness shall be heard in the light, all of which means that when he turned his request over to the darkness, his subconscious mind, where his idea gestated, the answer was presented full blown to him in due season.

There remaineth therefore a rest to the people of God. For he that is entered into his rest, he also hath ceased from his own works, as God did from his (Hebrews 4:9-10). The rest spoken of is your inner conviction—it is relaxation and a sense of indifference—it could be called the silent, inner knowing of the soul, your inner certitude, whereby you know your prayer is answered. When you are indifferent, you fail to react. You are indifferent when you are asleep. Divine indifference means you know it is impossible for your prayer to fail.

How She Practiced the Sabbath

A young woman had many dates and many disappointments. The men she went out with told her they were single but in time she discovered they were married and had lied to her and were just using her. Her two previous marriages had ended in divorce.

At my suggestion she practiced the following technique prior to sleep: She imagined I was shaking hands with her, wishing her all the blessings of life on her happy marriage. This meant to her that she was already married. She felt the solidity, naturalness and tangibility of the ring on her finger. All this took place in a passive, sleepy state every night, while she was fully conscious that she must first accept the ideal in her mind before any marriage could take place on the objective plane.

The ideal she had in mind was that of a spiritual minded man who harmonized with her perfectly. Hearing me wishing for her all the blessings of life every night was a means of impregnating her subconscious mind. Following this procedure, a short time afterward, she married a minister and was very happy. Become aware of the subtlety, the substantiality and the soundness of this simple technique.

She Worried Needlessly About Her Son

A mother was terribly troubled because her son cursed God and said, "There is no God." She had read in the Bible: *But he that shall blaspheme against the Holy Ghost hath never forgiveness, but is in danger of eternal damnation* (Mark 3:29).

This passage in the Bible has frightened many people. *Life, or God, however, is forever forgiving. Thou art of purer eyes than to be- hold evil, and canst not look on iniquity . . .* (Habakkuk 1:13). *For the Father judgeth no man, but hath committed all judgment unto the Son* (John 5:22).

The son means your mind, and you judge yourself by the thoughts you think and by the conclusions arrived at in your own mind. When you cease to criticize, castigate, demean and condemn yourself and enthrone God-like thoughts in your mind, there is an automatic response from your subconscious mind and the past is forgotten and remembered no more.

If you formerly misused or misapplied the principles of chemistry or mathematics and you now begin to use these principles in the right way, the principles of mathematics or chemistry have no grudge against you; likewise, your mind is a principle, and when you begin to use it in the right way you get immediate results. A new beginning is a new end. Begin with love and you end with success, health and peace of mind.

If a man refuses to seek guidance and inspiration or believes that he is incurable, he is simply shutting himself off from the Power of God to heal him, because his subconscious responds to his belief. For example, if you say that you know all the Truth and that there is nothing more to learn, then it will not be possible to cause you to see a greater measure of Truth, which is infinite in scope. As long as you refuse to forgive yourself and believe you are incurable or that the situation is hopeless, your attitude of mind is unforgivable while it lasts.

The Bible speaks in Oriental idiom and symbolic language, and to take the paragraph mentioned literally would be absurd.

When You Pray Don't Dwell on Time

And he looked up, and said, I see men as trees, walking. After that he put his hands again upon his eyes, and made him look up: and he was restored, and saw every man clearly (Mark 8:24-25).

Eyes in the Bible mean spiritual perception, an insight into the laws of mind. Man has dominion because he can exercise reflective control of his subconscious mind. For example, you can close your eyes now and sense and feel that you are already in the place you desire to be. You actualize the state not only by making there here but the future now. In your imagination you dramatize the state, and in that sensory vividness you open your eyes and you are amazed that you are not there. That means you have fixed the state in your subconscious mind and it will come to pass.

The Bible says, He looked up and saw men walking as trees. However, a tree does not walk; it is rooted in the soil and must wait for the various seasons to bring forth fruit. Man creates his own seasons and is not rooted like a tree. He doesn't have to wait for a healing of his eyes, or for health, love, peace or inspiration. God indwells him and is timeless and spaceless. Love is now; he can claim it now. Peace is now, and he can claim God's river of peace is flowing through him now. Strength is now, and he can claim that the Almighty Power is flowing through him now.

It is foolish to say, "Some day my eyes will be healed." The Infinite Healing Presence is within you. It is timeless and spaceless. Vision is spiritual, eternal and indestructible. Claim boldly, "My eyes are God's eyes and I see perfectly now." Why say, "Some day I will make my mark in the world?" Claim that Infinite Intelligence is guiding you now, this very minute, revealing to you your hidden talents and opening up a new door of expression for you. Cease postponing your good, for whatever you seek is within you as an idea, a thought or a principle, and everything you see in this world came out from either the mind of man or the mind of God. All inventions, discoveries and indeed everything you use in your workaday world came out of the mind of man. There is only One Source.

The Wonders of Prayer

For I say unto you, Among those that are born of women there is not a greater prophet than John the Baptist: but he that is least in the kingdom of God is greater than he (Luke 7:28).

This means that any man who prays successfully and touches Reality is greater than the so-called wisest man in the world. One man may be wise in the ways of the world and be completely governed by his five senses; the other man knows how to contact the Infinite within him and find peace in this changing world.

The Meaning of Our Father

After this manner therefore pray ye: Our Father which art in heaven . . . (Matthew 6:9).

Our Father means that all of us have a common progenitor—the Life Principle—and we are all intimately related. Actually, we are all brothers and sisters. The word *humanity* means the One Being appearing as many. This indicates your essential unity with God, with all men and with all things in the world. There is but One Mind and One Spirit animating all of us.

When you pray, it is essential that you have a sense of unity with all men and women and with all things in the world. All things—all the beasts of the field and the fowl of the air—came forth from the One Source, and one part of Spirit cannot be antagonistic to another part of Spirit, as Spirit is one and indivisible. When you say *Our Father*, you realize the great law of unity or oneness. This reduces all sense of conflict and releases the imprisoned splendor within you.

Learn to Become Aware

You must be conscious of a state to witness it. A man who never saw an electric switch or a telephone cannot distinguish between the two, because he is not aware of them. Become aware of the Indwelling God within you and claim that what is true of God is also true of you, and wonders will happen in your life.

God is in the murderer as well as in the holy man. God is not less in one than the other. God is, and cannot become greater or lesser. The murderer can be transformed when he has a hunger and thirst to become a new man. As he saturates his mind and heart with the great eternal verities and absorbs and incorporates these truths in his soul, he becomes transformed and is a new man in God. The law of the subconscious is compulsive; whereas before he was compelled to do evil, now he is compelled to do good.

The Wonders of Faith in God

Now faith is the substance of things hoped for, the evidence of things not seen (Hebrews 11:1). *But without faith it is impossible to please him: for he that cometh to God must believe that he is, and that he is a rewarded of them that diligently seek him* (Hebrews 11:6).

At the New Thought Convention held in Chicago under the auspices of Rev. Johnnie Coleman, Minister of Unity Foundation for Better Living, I was one of many speakers. After a two-hour session with a group of students, one of the listeners told me that his grandfather was a bushman. As a young boy he had climbed on board an English ship and a Scottish sailor took him back to England. He was educated and later became a distinguished clergyman in England, demonstrating that when the boy from Africa was exposed to a spiritual atmosphere and a wonderful, peaceful environment and taught a reverence for the Divinity within him, he became transformed. He was known as the cultured, soft spoken, gentle, spiritual giant; yet he had been a bushman. The grandson who told me this story said that the Scotchman was deeply religious and had faith that the boy he adopted would express the Divinity within in a wonderful way, and the Infinite responded according to his faith.

By faith Enoch was translated that he should not see death; and was not found, because God had translated him: for before his translation he had this testimony, that he pleased God (Hebrews 11:5).

Enoch means any man's present state of mind. When you get into a mood or conviction, you translate or supplant the old mood and mental attitude and you are different. The old state of mind can't be found. You can't see a conviction. Where is the cripple whom you visited in the hospital? He now walks upright and is successful in all his undertakings.

Recently I visited a home for senior citizens and talked with a man who had lost the use of his legs. His son said to me, "If you will talk with him and teach him how to pray, he has great faith, I am sure he will get up and walk." The prayer I gave him was very simple: "God walks and talks in me, and through the Power of the Almighty I am made whole." I also told him to picture himself walking into my home to tell me about the miracle that happened and to imagine and feel that I was greeting him and congratulating him on the miracle God had wrought. He was to make there here and the future now in his imagination, and he was to feel the reality of it all. In other words, mentally and emotionally, and in his imagery, he was in my study and he felt my imaginary handshake.

He repeated this over and over again many times a day until he felt the naturalness and sensory vividness of it all. A month later he walked in on a Monday morning and experienced objectively what he had been dramatizing in his mind many times a day for four weeks. He translated the old, crippled state to the man walking uprightly in the law. He died to the old state, and you cannot find the crippled state no matter where you look.

It Was Written by Men

New Bibles are being constantly brought forth and previous errors in translation are being corrected and modified. The Bible, being written by men, is not perfect, and numerous errors have been discovered from time to time. What we must learn is not the letter or the word—the word is the mood, the thought-feeling, the inner meaning it conveys. Many people believe you must quote the Bible word for word. How can you? The original Bible was not written in English; and the original Hebrew of 5000 years ago is entirely different from modern Hebrew, just as the language of Chaucer is vastly different from the English of today.

In this day and age, you would not call your daughter Daisy, Fannie or Pansy—words, through the passage of time, change their meaning. When I was a boy these names for girls were commonplace. Nor would you call your son Judas, because you would not want your son to be ridiculed at school.

We are not dealing with words here, but with moods. For example, the word John means love; Peter means faith in the One God; James means righteous judgment, i.e., coming to a decision based on eternal truths, which are the same yesterday, today and forever. The word sin means a missing of the mark, failing to realize your desire in life. You are really sinning when you fail to lead a full and happy life. The word Judas means lack, limitation, your personal problem. We are all born with Judas; i.e., we are born into all that our environment represents. We came from the limitless state and find ourselves now in a three-dimensional world. We are here to discover who we are. Through problems, difficulties and challenges, we discover our Divinity. Our joy is in overcoming.

The men who translated the Bible had to capture the moods of the mystics who wrote the book thousands of years ago. They had a partial key—not the entire key. In the King James version, you read: *The fear of the Lord is the beginning of knowledge* . . . (Proverbs 1:7). The Bible also says that God is love. All this really seems contradictory.

In the days when the King James version was written, however, fear meant to have a healthy, reverent respect for the Lord, or the Law, in the same way you should have a reverent respect for the laws of chemistry or electricity; otherwise, you would get into a lot of trouble.

The English of the Magna Carta, that wonderful document, is unreadable and cannot be understood unless you have mastered the English language of that period.

Whose Wife Shall She Be?

The same day came to him the Sadducees, which say that there isno resurrection, and asked him, Saying, Master, Moses said, If a man die, having no children, his brother shall marry his wife, and raise up seed unto his brother.

Now there were with us seven brethren: and the first, when he had married a wife, deceased, and, having no issue, left his wife unto his brother:

Likewise, the second also, and the third, unto the seventh. And last of all the woman died also.

Therefore in the resurrection whose wife shall she be of the seven? for they all had her.

Jesus answered and said unto them, Ye do err, not knowing the scriptures, nor the power of God.

For in the resurrection they neither marry, nor are given in marriage, but are as the angels of God in heaven (Matthew 22:23-30).

If a man is married now and he believes in reincarnation, he must have thousands of wives. Which one is his? Likewise, he must have thousands of mothers and fathers. Which mother is his? Man misses the point altogether. The belief in reincarnation is a solace, an opiate, a sort of narcotic to the individual who has met with many defeats, and the belief is a comfort to him. The theory pleases his vanity and exalts his ego.

If an individual who has now hit the bottom is told in hypnotic regression that he was once famous, he likes to hear that his misfortunes are due to his karma and misdeeds in a former life. Tell a man that when he forgives himself, his sins are forgiven him. Man should stop punishing himself, as God punishes no man.

I have written about the subject of reincarnation somewhat at length in the last chapter of *Psychic Perception*. I might add, however, that the reason the modern theory of reincarnation is popular is because man, using his five senses only, is like the five foolish virgins: he has no oil or wisdom in his lamps. He finds that the explanation that he comes back again and again on this plane to expiate for his former sins gives him some solace and tells him what he wants to hear.

At the same time it seems to unfold many unexplained phenomena. Such acceptance retards spiritual progress, checks the awakening process and is a destructive, superstitious belief. Mozart, Lincoln, Shakespeare and countless others left their impressions with mankind. We read of their works in history, song and prose. All of them live in the hearts or subjective minds of men.

When husband and wife enter into the creative act, they can give conception to any state they are capable of conceiving. The dominant mood will prevail, as the subconscious mind always accepts the dominant mood or feeling. If they dwell on and admire the qualities and attributes of Lincoln and would love to give birth to such a son ("as within, so without,"), then a child is born with these qualities; but it is not Lincoln coming back again. It is the tone struck during conception, or creation, that determines the nature of the child. This is plain common sense. It is the law of mind in action.

Now, to come back to the question asked by the Sadducees, who were a religious sect with strong materialistic beliefs but without spiritual understanding. They looked upon the marriage spoken of as a physical marriage. The Bible is speaking of mental and spiritual things, of the psychological and spiritual man, who makes many mental and emotional unions called marriages in this world.

Likewise, in the *I Ching* a marriage means embracing or believing in an idea or opinion. If you believe strawberries give you hives, that is a marriage, Biblically speaking, and you have an issue from it; namely, the physical result of the belief or opinion embraced by you. If you marry or embrace the idea that sitting near a fan will give you a stiff neck, you will have an issue from that marriage; namely, a stiff neck. Look at the countless mental marriages men make in this world, embracing and accepting all sorts of false beliefs, opinions and superstitions.

Paul said: . . . *I die daily* (I Corinthians 15:31). You must die to what you are now so that you can live to what you want to be. You are in heaven now; it is not some place you go when you die. You live, move and have your being in that Infinite Spirit within you, which was never born and will never die. You can die to fear and live in faith in God and all things good. You can die to poverty and live in God's riches, which are all around you. You can die to superstitions and embrace the wisdom of God, thereby experiencing the second birth, a spiritual regeneration in which the wisdom of God anoints your intellect, and you think, speak and act from the standpoint of the Infinite Presence and Power; not the superimposed structure of ignorance, fear and superstition, which are called the three ruffians.

Some months ago I counseled an alcoholic who had lost his family, his business and his prestige. He was completely irresponsible and full of self-condemnation. He decided to die to his present state and go to heaven; namely, harmony, health, peace and accomplishment.

Every night he decreed: "Peace and sobriety are mine now. The Almighty Power flows through me, giving me freedom, peace, harmony and strength. I have made a decision and I know the Power of God will back me up." At the end of a week he was completely free from the habit. He came to a decision to become a new man, went back to his wife and children, attended night school, and began to apply himself with tenacity to classes on business management.

His industry and zeal has paid off. He is now conducting his own business and is a wonderful success. He died psychologically to the sick man, the weak man, the insecure, whining and complaining man, and was reborn to peace, tranquility, triumph and accomplishment. Psychologically, he died and went to heaven (peace and harmony).

The inner meaning of the Bible makes sense: *The letter killeth, but the spirit giveth life* (II Corinthians 3:6).

4

Things You Want to Know

And the devil said unto him, If thou be the Son of God, command this stone that it be made bread. And Jesus answered him, saying, It is written, That man shall not live by bread alone, but by every word of God (Luke 4:34).

This could be looked at as the tempter's attitude; in other words, if you have all this God-Power within you, you might throw yourself from the mountain top and nothing will happen to you. The tempter, taunting you, also says to you: Let's see you heal the cripple, the blind man, the man where cancer has metastasized all over his system.

When you say, "I must prove it to myself first," you are trying to project a state of mind which you do not have. You are entertaining a mood of doubt. At the same time you wish to express a mood of faith or conviction. You are tempting the Infinite. You are deviating from the law of mind, which, as you know, means that whatever you impress in your subconscious comes forth according to the nature of the impression. Electricity does not bend to your whims; it operates from a higher to a lower potential and will operate for you when you understand the principles of electricity.

And the devil, taking him up into an high mountain, shewed unto him all the kingdoms of the world in a moment of time. And the devil said unto him, All this power will I give thee . . . If thou therefore wilt worship me, all shall be thine (Luke 4:5-7).

The devil, or Satan, means to deviate from the truth or to judge according to appearances. For example, if you should visit a sick friend in the hospital who has a loathsome disease and you begin to fear that you may get it, your devil is that negative thought beguiling you to turn away from the idea of wholeness, beauty and perfection. The Spirit in you is ever perfect, and your thought should be on the immaculate, unblemished Presence of God in you.

Man is inclined to worship power, and when he gets it, somehow he gets the idea that he has the Divine right of Kings and forgets the real Source of power. *Then saith Jesus unto him, Get thee hence, Satan: for it is written, Thou shall worship the Lord thy God, and him only shalt thou serve* (Matthew 4:10). You are to give all your allegiance, loyalty and devotion to the Spirit within—the Source of all your blessings; your security and protection.

He Used Power Wisely

President Lincoln used the powers of his office wisely. During much of his lifetime he was maligned and traduced. Many in high places did everything in their power to derogate his reputation. Many men, when they are in positions of power and prestige, abuse their power. They begin to think that the power was given to them because they were personally great; that their judgment is supreme and that they cannot err. Moreover, they want no interference. This attitude fails them, however, because they forget that the real power is within, and that man is great only when he aligns himself with the Infinite and permits himself to be a channel for the light, the wisdom and the power of the Infinite One. The wise man like Lincoln looks for guidance and direction from God within him, and he does not flamboyantly flaunt his power in front of others. On the contrary, he is humble, kind and has a deep reverence for the Divinity which shapes our ends.

Who Is Boss?

You are all familiar with the type of man who gets promoted and says, "I'll show them who is boss. I'll let them all know." He is very insecure and feels inadequate to the job; therefore, he strives to make up for the sense of lack within himself by an ostentatious show of power, which betrays him.

The Origin and Meaning of the Word, "Devil"

Organized religion has always accounted for the presence of evil in the world by inventing a devil. The Bible points out clearly the answer: *I form the light, and create darkness: I make peace, and create evil: I the Lord do all these things* (Isaiah 45:7).

Again occur the curious words: And the Lord (the law of his subconscious) hardened Pharaoh's heart. Pharaoh, by his hostility and hatred, hardened his own heart. His subconscious responded to his mental attitude. All this is very simple when you understand it. There is but one Power. *Hear, O Israel: the Lord our God is one Lord* (Deuteronomy 6:4). Not two or three or a thousand; just one.

When you use the One Power ignorantly, stupidly, negatively or maliciously, people call it the devil, Satan, misery, suffering, lack and limitation. When you use the One Power constructively, harmoniously and wisely, people call it God, Allah, Brahma, health, happiness, peace and prosperity.

You can use any power in nature two ways. You can use electricity to fry an egg or to electrocute someone. You can use water to quench the thirst of your child or to drown the child. The same wind that blows a ship onto the rocks will also take it to safety. The forces of nature are not evil; it depends upon how you use them.

The word "devil" means of evil, or "a spirit of evil"—not *the* Spirit of evil—such as hate, jealousy, hostility, resentment, ill will, vengeance, etc. These are the mental attitudes or devils that bedevil man. The theological devil was invented by the church.

God Upside Down

The ancient Hebrew mystics taught that the devil is God upside-down. In other words, it is man's twisted, distorted, morbid concept of the Divine Presence. He has made God in his own image and likeness and has projected his own animosities, jealousies, shortcomings, prejudices and derelictions onto a God of love.

To put the whole thing in simple language that a boy of eight could understand, the devil is God as he is misunderstood by the ignorant masses. The devil of the theologian is purely personification. It has no existence.

Only One Power

Scientifically, mathematically and spiritually, there can be only One Power. If there were two powers, one would cancel out the other. There would be no order, design, symmetry or proportion in the world. There would be a clash, and only chaos would prevail. It is a cosmos; not a chaos. Reverse the word *evil* and you have *live*, meaning to live life backwards. Your evil is going against the stream of life, which moves forward harmoniously, peacefully, joyously and rhythmically.

Stop living life backwards. Progress with the great stream of life, the tendency or will of which always brings a greater measure of life, love, truth, beauty and abundance. All things, all processes and all activities are from One Source. It must, therefore, follow that there can be no evil in the Absolute. Our evil comes from misapplication, misinterpretation, and lack of understanding of the nature of the One Power. Our evil is our ignorance, our incomplete state of consciousness, from our seeing things in the wrong light. That which man calls evil in humans he does not call evil in animals, which are governed by natural instincts.

You Are Here to Discover Yourself

You are a choosing and volitional being. You are here to discover yourself and reveal the Divinity within. Problems, challenges and difficulties enable you to sharpen your mental and spiritual tools and grow spiritually. God becomes man for the joy of discovering Himself. You are that man, and you are capable of reproducing all the qualities, attributes and potencies of God. *I have said, Ye are gods; and all of you are children of the most High* (Psalms 82:6).

The Simple Truth

The Greek word for *devil* is *diabolos*—one who throws obstacles across. These obstacles or difficulties are stepping stones to our triumph and accomplishment. The joy is in overcoming. All progress in the world comes from people who succeed in overcoming their obstacles. The ancient Hebrew mystics referred to the devil as mirth or laughter, for one of the "amusing" things about this so-called devil (which never existed and was invented by the church) is that he looms larger and gets greater attention than God in the minds of millions.

He Said He Was a Hell-Dodger

While holding a consultation with an alcoholic, he said to me: "I go to church not to go to heaven, but to escape from hell. I'm a hell-dodger." He had learned that man creates his own hell (misery and suffering) and his own heaven (his mind at peace). I explained to him how George Bernard Shaw strikingly illustrated man's weird superstitious beliefs in "Man and Superman," where Donna Ann cries out indignantly when she finds herself in hell: "I in hell? I, a faithful daughter of the church, who has kept all her fasts and denied myself all pleasure? And I might *have* had such a good time. Oh, there is some mistake!"

Other Meanings

The word *devil* means also *slanderer*, *liar*, or one who tells lies about God. One of the Hebrew words for the devil was Ayin, which means the eye. The eye slanders the fact for the simple reason that it deals with external appearances, which oftentimes are very deceptive. For example, people say, "The sun rises." They also say, "The sun sets," "The earth is flat," and "The sun moved around the earth." Yet all this is completely false.

We see nothing as it really is. Our eyes are geared to see three dimensionally only. When you see clairvoyantly you see things differently. When you begin to see spiritually and in mystic illumination, you will look at a tree and see waves of light. You will immediately perceive the whole world as a universe of densities, frequencies and intensities. Hence, the Hebrew attribution of mirth to the word Ayin, which means the eyes.

The Revealing Truth of Ancient Symbolism

A few years ago at a seminar on the sea, I drew on a blackboard the symbolism of the devil as portrayed by ancient Hebrew mystics. It is a creature that never possibly could have existed—the product of primitive man's ignorance and distorted imagination. The devil was depicted as having goat's horns, a man's head with donkey's ears, the wings of a bat, the upper part of the body human, the thighs those of an animal, and the legs human though ending in eagle's claws.

If you have a deck of Tarot cards designed by Pamela Colman Smith under the instruction of Arthur Edward Waite, published by University Books, New Hyde Park, New York, you could look at the symbolism of the card marked *devil* and you would find it very amusing, illuminating and instructive.

Bat wings signify darkness and gross ignorance.

The horns are those of a goat and suggest no backbone, which means that man's animal propensities and passions are not controlled, subdued or sublimated spiritually, which they should be. Man is here to walk uprightly in the Law, and when his backbone is curved, he can't walk or stand erect.

The head has donkey ears, indicating the obtuseness and stubbornness of man, who refuses to listen to the guidance of the Infinite Presence and Power within him.

The human part of his body is very gross, indicating the absence of grace, beauty and Divine order.

The thighs are animal-like, indicating animal passions and appetites, lust, greed, etc. He is driven by instinct rather than by spiritual impulses, which are lying dormant within him. Man is here to stir up the gift of God within him.

The legs are human. They portray and indicate that the animal passions are driving the human part instead of the other way about, as it should be.

The legs end in eagles' claws. This is subtle symbolism and indicates misuse of the sex urge, such as sexual aberrations and perversions along all lines.

The pentagram over the head is inverted. The five-pointed star symbolizes the spiritual minded man and stands on two points, the conscious and subconscious, harmonized and balanced. Here it stands only on one point, however, indicating he is completely unbalanced and wallowing in negative emotions and destructive sensations.

The torch symbolizes that he is constantly inflaming his passions and toward sexual deviations. The left shoulder of the woman in the card is lacking, and the left shoulder of the man is developed out of proportion. The shoulders are the indices of emotions, and his emotions pander to his abnormal sensations, robbing himself of vitality, enthusiasm and energy.

The man and woman depicted in the card have horns, hoofs and tail, and signify they are living with their animal passions and appetites. The tail is shaped like a scorpion, symbolic of bestiality and sexual abnormalities. The bunch of grapes indicates that the subconscious expresses what is impressed upon it—the desire of your conscious mind, when impregnated in the subconscious, brings forth the fruit and result of your desires.

The devil has a navel, as also have the man and the woman. This reveals the whole story and is a profound and subtle symbol. It indicates that all are man-made.

From the above illustration, you will immediately perceive that the devil is man himself, as he misuses the law and misdirects the God-given life force. No wonder the Hebrew mystics said the devil is God Upside Down.

Learn to Exalt God in the Midst of You

Every time you are prone to criticize, demean or demote yourself, affirm immediately: "I exalt God in the midst of me." You can't think of two things at the same time, and as you continue regularly and systematically to exalt God in the midst of you, you are injecting that idea into your subconscious mind. After a while, it will become automatic and you cease all self-condemnation and self-criticism. It is important to stress dignity and respect, however, because man's self-respect is his greatest asset.

You Can't Buy Respect

Some men think they can buy respect and dignity. They can't. For example, the late Mussolini knew he did not have the dignity of Haile Selassie, who was a king, and when he came to London he came as a king. He said, "I am a king and I will return to my land as a king and conqueror." Mussolini would have loved to have had the same honor and prestige, but he did not feel it and could not claim it in consciousness. Haile Selassie felt the honor and dignity in his mentality and received it, accordingly. Mussolini lost prestige and died in disgrace. Hitler also strutted before his generals, seized power and demanded recognition and honor; but all the time he was deeply conscious of his inferiority, inadequacy and insecurity.

There are men who think they can buy their way into a select club and that they can thus buy respect. They can't. The bell boy, the waiter and the doorman give more respect to the member of the club who can barely pay his dues, because he has the consciousness of being a dignified person and demands respect. He is conscious of the Divine Self within him and of his kingship in the conceptive realm of his mind.

Walk the Earth a Queen

The queen is not conscious of doing wrong, even though what she does may be contrary to your religious beliefs and traditional concept of things. She is free from censure and a sense of guilt and walks the earth in a high and exalted mood. A woman who said she belonged to a particular religious group said to me that she was shocked to see a certain queen drink, smoke and eat meat. All this is, of course, utter nonsense and too ridiculous for words.

Paul says, *I know, and am persuaded by the Lord Jesus that there is nothing unclean of itself, but to him that esteemeth anything to be unclean, to him it is unclean* (Romans 14:14) . . . *I considered, and saw four-footed beasts of the earth, and wild beasts, and creeping things, and fowls of the air. And I heard a voice saying unto me, Arise, Peter; slay and eat. But I said, Not so, Lord: for nothing common or unclean hath at any time entered into my mouth. But the voice answered me again from heaven, What God hath cleansed, that call not thou common. And this was done three times* . . . (Acts 11:6-10).

Things are clean or unclean according to your concept of yourself. If you have made a law for yourself and if you believe that taking a cocktail is injurious or interferes with your spiritual growth, you should follow your code or belief, because with that kind of belief your subconscious responds according to the nature of your belief. To you it would be wrong. Likewise, if you have made a law for yourself that it is wrong and injurious to your spiritual unfoldment to eat meat, you again have made that law for yourself and you should, therefore, follow it. If you break the code you have established for yourself, you will feel guilty and suffer accordingly. There is nothing good or bad, but thinking makes it so. There is no guilt but the consciousness of guilt.

He Wondered Why His Wife Left Him

While talking with a man after the sermon one Sunday morning, he said his wife had packed up and left a note saying she could no longer put up with his negative vibrations and low estimate of himself. During the conversation I discovered that his wife was a brilliant woman, possessing a Ph.D. degree, and being very successful professionally. He was a salesman in the vitamin field and also doing well financially.

The real cause of the marital break was that he felt he was not good enough for her, and he was constantly thinking and fearing that she would surely find someone else. He went to sleep in that mood of fear every night, and his subconscious gave back to him what he ordered and requested, as it never makes a mistake. Actually, he brought it to pass by his constant fear . . . *The thing which I greatly feared is come upon me* (Job 3:25).

His wife mirrored his conception of himself, and she testified to his state of consciousness. His mood of self-depreciation and inferiority plus his subconscious belief that she would leave him was communicated to her subconsciously, and she, not knowing the laws of mind and not being spiritually oriented, responded accordingly.

At my suggestion, he phoned her and explained what he had been doing, stating that the whole thing was his fault. Both are now reconciled and are practicing prayer-therapy night and morning. Every night prior to sleep, he affirms out loud: "The Spirit in me talks to the Spirit of my wife, and there are harmony, love, peace, joy and understanding between us. The Light of God shines in her, and whenever I think of her, I immediately affirm, 'I exalt God in the midst of you.' Whenever I am prone, because of habit, to demean or demote myself, I will affirm, 'I exalt God in the midst of me. I am God's son, and God loves me and cares for me.'"

Likewise, every morning his wife affirmed out loud: "My husband is God's man. I salute the Divinity in him. There are peace, love, harmony and understanding between us. He is growing in wisdom, truth and love. Whenever I think of him during the day, I will immediately affirm, 'God loves him and cares for him.'"

True love is an irrepressible inclination and impulse to give. Both are giving out more life, love, truth and beauty to each other, and the marriage is growing more blessed and beautiful as time goes on. Love is the universal solvent. Love frees; it heals; it is the Spirit of God, for God is love.

5

Your Business Is God's Business

. . . *Wist ye not that I must be about my Father's business?* (Luke 2:49). My Father's business is a greater measure of livingness and givingness. You are here to lead a full and happy life and to express your talents at the highest possible level. In other words, you are here to lead the abundant life—full of joy and beauty. You may magnify and increase your powers by constantly claiming morning, noon and night: "I am releasing more and more of God's love, light, truth and beauty every moment of the day." As you make a habit of this affirmation, you will be amazed at the wonders that will happen in your life, and the whole world will be blessed because you walked this way, radiating the sunshine of God's love.

Cease Forcing Your Opinion on Others

A young girl was trying to convert all members of her family to the study of the science of mind. They resented her and rejected all her statements and even refused to read the literature she proffered them. This is the wrong approach. Let the other person alone. Do not try to mentally coerce him to your way of thinking. Cease thinking about all the differences in religious beliefs, but, instead, consider the fundamental unity of all religions. A man's religion is his relationship with God. If it makes him happy and contented and he gets comfort from his beliefs, don't try to force your opinion on him.

Lutheran Girl Healed by a Unity Minister

While conversing with a Unity minister, she told me that a Lutheran girl who was very ill in the hospital had asked her to come and pray with her, which she did. The Unity minister said to her, "Join your hands in mine and we will pray to Jesus to heal you." The girl was completely healed. You might call this blind faith. It was the subconscious belief of the Lutheran girl that brought about the healing.

There is only One Healing Power, and It is available to all. That Healing Power is in the subconscious of every living person. Results follow according to the belief of the person doing the praying. Many people believe in a personal Jesus to heal or a personal Buddha. They get results because of their beliefs. Whether the object of your faith be true or false, you will get results because of the sincerity of your belief and not because of the thing believed in. There are many people who believe in the usage of amulets, talismans and sacred relics for healing purposes. They get results also.

The Right Approach

If a person is ill, don't say to him: "You had the wrong thoughts. Your religious belief is all wrong." You will only make him worse. If he is willing to listen, teach him about the wonders of the healing powers within him and how to use his mind constructively. Don't take a man's creed or religious beliefs away from him unless you give him something better instead—something he can use, thereby becoming a greater, grander, nobler and more dignified character.

Looking Behind the Symbols

Behind all the religions of the world you will find the underlying truth, but the truth has been covered all over with a thick cloud of rituals, ceremonies, symbols, liturgies and various interpretations. There is only One Truth, and God is Truth, which is the same yesterday, today and forever. Unfortunately, the eternal verities and the principles of life are lost in creedal dogmas.

They Get Answers Also

People's prayers are answered in orthodox churches, also. It is much better, however, to know the laws of mind and learn to use scientific prayer. It would be unkind to take away all of man's beliefs and to give him nothing instead. Man will accept this new teaching which I am writing about when he is ready, but he can't be coerced into receiving it.

She Was Afraid of Black Magic

Surely there is no enchantment against Jacob, neither is there any divination against Israel: according to this time it shall be said of Jacob and of Israel, What hath God wrought! (Numbers 23:23).

A young girl working in an office was told that another girl was practicing black magic against her. I explained to her, however, that what people call black magic is an inversion of the law of God, which is all-good. If I wish another person evil, I must be in a very negative state myself; therefore, I bring evil on myself and will be stricken, as my moods are creative. The only way my negative thought can hurt the other is for the other person to foolishly and stupidly accept my suggestion and grant me the power to injure him. Then the other person will become the victim. But if the other person should laugh at me and at my supposed power, then all the negative thoughts would boomerang back to me, all of which would be self-destructive.

The voodoo doctor in Australia and/or the jungles of Africa always sends his intended prey a message informing him of the fact that his image is being burned. The victim becomes panic stricken and the fear engendered by himself kills him. Man actualizes black magic by believing in it. Although the other person is working negatively against you, pouring out imprecations and execrations upon you and visualizing you as dead, in reality he is unable to do so, because he doesn't want death for himself. I advised a man, for example, to cease wishing death for his wife. (They hated each other.) He refused the advice and he died shortly after. The wife, though, is still living and prospering.

Remember, if you are walking in the consciousness of God's love, the low or negative vibrations of the mass mind cannot touch you. All of us are subject to the negative vibrations, i.e., fears and anxieties of the mass mind. If you are prayed up, they do not hurt you; you shake them off and become impervious to them. You cannot attract that which you are unlike. You only draw into your experience that which is compatible with your moods and state of consciousness.

Walk with God at all times, realizing that God is sovereign, supreme, your ruler, guide and counselor; and *nothing shall by any means hurt you* (Luke 10:19). *They shall not hurt nor destroy in all my holy mountain, saith the Lord* (Isaiah 65:25). *Thou art my hiding place; thou shalt preserve me from trouble; thou shalt compass me about with songs of deliverance* (Psalm 32:7). *Surely there is no enchantment against Jacob* (a man aware of the One Power—God), *neither is there any divination against Israel* (a man ruled by God, who recognizes the sovereignty of the Spirit) (Numbers 23:23). *Because thou hast made the Lord, which is my refuge, even the most High, thy habitation; there shall no evil befall thee, neither shall any plague come nigh thy dwelling* (Psalm 91:9-10).

The Door to True Expression

Verily, verily, I say unto you, He that entereth not by the door into the sheepfold, but climbeth up some other way, the same is a thief and a robber. But he that entereth in by the door is the shepherd of the sheep (John 10:1-2).

I AM is the door. This means your own consciousness is the door to all expression. In other words, you must have the mental equivalent established in your subconscious mind in order to manifest what you desire and what you want to achieve in life. When you try to accomplish on the outside what you have not felt as true on the inside, you will fail, e.g., when a man claims to be something other than what he really feels himself to be, such as claiming that he is a great actor when in his heart he does not feel it to be true, he is robbing himself and is the thief mentioned in the above verses.

He must claim and honestly feel himself to be the great actor and, further, dramatize the role; and as he continues to claim and feel that he is the great actor, the power of the subconscious will back him up and he will manifest the role. The embodied states of mind are the sheep mentioned. The feeling of being what you long to be must always precede the embodied state, resulting in the manifestation of what is felt as true subjectively.

And when he putteth forth his own sheep, he goeth before them, and the sheep follow him: for they know his voice. And a stranger will they not follow, but will flee from him: for they know not the voice of strangers (John 10:4-5).

You are a stranger when you are simply stating in words that you are rich and prosperous when actually you are not. The sheep (the lovely states you wish to embody) will not follow you. You are merely boasting and masquerading, and the sheep do not hear that voice because it is not the true voice.

You must come to a clear-cut decision that God is the real source of your supply, that His riches are circulating in your life and that there is always a Divine surplus. Write these truths with your conscious mind into your subconscious. You do this by repetition, faith in the laws of your mind, and a joyous expectancy, while knowing that whatever you convey to or impress on your subconscious will come forth pressed down, shaken together and running over. You must feel the truth of what you affirm. Your subconscious accepts your conviction. What you really believe in your conscious mind will be accepted by your subconscious mind.

Mere verbalisms are not enough. Many people claim prosperity, success and wealth, but their subconscious belief is really in lack, limitation and failure. Your conscious and subconscious must synchronize and agree. When the two agree, your prayer is answered. Reason things out and you will find it is not difficult to realize that God is the only Source of health, wealth, peace and inspiration, and, indeed, all things. There is only One Source. Everything you look at came out of the mind of man or the mind of the Infinite. Wealth is a state of mind; poverty is a state of mind. It is done unto you as you believe.

All that ever came before me are thieves and robbers: but the sheep did not hear them (John 10:8). One time I heard a clergyman say to an audience that the meaning of this paragraph in the Book of John was that all religions before Christianity were false. This obviously is the quintessence of absurdity and stupidity, for . . . *God is no respecter of persons* (Acts 10:34).

There is an old Hindu aphorism which says: "When you name It, you cannot find It; and when you find It, you cannot name It." How could you label love, peace, joy, happiness, inspiration, guidance, goodwill, compassion, mercy, kindness, illumination or laughter? Any man who walks the earth may contact the God-Presence and receive an answer. The God-Presence will respond to any man's prayer, regardless of creedal affiliations. God answers the prayer of the atheist also, who says there is no God.

The man who believes in the goodness of God in the land of the living, and who lives in the joyous expectancy of the best in life, has true faith. The man who doubts the love, the joy and the wonders of the Infinite and who disbelieves in the response of the Infinite to his own thought is the real atheist.

Explanation of John 10:8

Do not let anything come before your belief in the Power of the Almighty working in your behalf. For example, if you believe that outside conditions, people, circumstances or current events preclude your possibilities of fulfilling your desires, you are greatly mistaken and are living as a thief and a robber, because you are robbing yourself of the joy of the answered prayer. You are saying that conditions and people are greater than God, which is absurd. In other words, you are making gods of other people and you are, therefore, unjust to yourself. There is nothing to oppose Omnipotence; nothing to thwart It or to vitiate It. It is Almighty, and there is no other power.

The Crossroads of Life

. . . *Go your way into the village over against you: and as soon as ye be entered into it, ye shall find a colt tied, whereon never man sat; loose him, and bring him* (Mark 11:2). *And they went their way, and found the colt tied by the door without in a place where two ways met; and they loose him* (Mark 11:4). *And they brought the colt to Jesus, and cast their garments on him; and he sat upon him* (Mark 11:7).

All of us are at the crossroads every day. The colt at the crossroads is your mood—your mental and emotional state—before entering into the deep of yourself. The colt represents the undisciplined state. Suppose you have a desire to sing and you have a wonderful voice, but you fail to have an outlet for your voice on the stage or radio. You must then discipline yourself and affirm knowingly: "God gave me this voice, and God opens the perfect channel for me where He sings majestic cadences through me." Imagine you are before the microphone or on the stage singing gloriously and majestically before an imaginary audience. Feel the thrill and joy and wonder of it all. Practice running this mental movie frequently in your mind. As you continue to do it, you are disciplining the colt (the formerly undisciplined desire), and your mental image, through frequent habitations of the mind, will sink into your subconscious and come to pass in Divine order.

The crossroads also indicate our capacity to choose, divide and select. Watch what you take into the deep of yourself every night. As you go to sleep, your conscious and subconscious are creatively joined together, and your last waking concept is registered in your subconscious. In other words, your conscious mood prior to sleep has crossed over to your subconscious mind and the latter brings it to pass, whether good or bad. Your reactions to today's impressions mold your tomorrows. Be careful of your reactions, as these are the moods or tones which, if carried into the deeper mind, will manifest themselves.

You can control your reactions and thereby control your moods. They brought the colt to Jesus. One of the meanings of Jesus in the Bi- ble is "illumined reason." It also means "I AM," *Je Suis* in French. The names Jesus and Joshua in the Old Testament are identical. Both mean God is the Savior, or solution to all problems. And, of course, you know God indwells you, and you are your own savior.

The word Jesus also means your desire, the realization of which would save you from any predicament. You bring your desire to the I AM, your consciousness, within you; and as you feel the reality of it and rejoice that the Almighty Power is moving in your behalf, and as you sustain this mood, which is the meaning of He sat upon the colt, you ride the mood, this means that you remain faithful to your desire until you reach Jerusalem, which means the city of peace, or the impregnation of your subconscious. After the impregnation of your subconscious, your desire, like a seed, undergoes dissolution and you experience the manifestation of your ideal. This is the meaning of . . . *And Jesus entered into Jerusalem* . . .

And in the morning, as they passed by, they saw the fig tree dried up from the roots. And Peter calling to remembrance saith unto him, Master, behold, the fig tree which thou cursedst is withered away (Mark 11:20-21).

A complete rejection of lack, a refusal to accept limitation or the acceptance of failure withers the idea of lack away.

. . . *No man eat fruit of thee hereafter forever* . . . (Mark 11:14).

This means there will be no acceptance of doubt hereafter and no acknowledgement of lack. The fig tree in the Bible is a symbol of lack, sorrow and limitation.

Perpetual Motion

Men talk of perpetual motion. It can never be accomplished mechanically. The only perpetual motion is your consciousness, your awareness, your I AMness. This is Self-Existence and is eternal; it requires no other power. It is the initial velocity or vibration; therefore, all other vibrations are lesser vibrations of the One. They are modifications of the Only Presence and the Only Power. For example, if you fix something in your mind now, it is arrested in its motion and is attached or impressed in your subconscious and will be objectified. Two things cannot occupy the same place at the same time: The old state passes away.

A woman, for example, tried to sell her apartment building for several weeks. One night she quieted her mind and in her imagination took a prospective buyer through the building, showing him the financial books and all the facilities of the building. She heard him say, "I'll take it." She heard this over and over again as she went to sleep. In the morning she felt at peace. The motion in her mind regarding selling it had ceased. She had succeeded in a subjective embodiment of her desire and was at peace about it. She had no further desire to pray about it. That same day a man came in, looked the property over and accepted it. The price was right, the buyer was right and the time was right.

The Power of Blind Belief

On one of my trips to Europe, I met a distant relative, who told me of a very interesting experience which he had had. His father was dying of cancer, and he came home from Australia to visit him. When he saw his father, he said to him: "Dad, I brought something wonderful for you—a piece of the true cross. It has healed many people. I can't keep it; I must return it to the Bishop who loaned it to me for a large sum of money, in order to heal you." He touched his father with this supposedly true cross. That night his father slept with this splinter of wood on his chest and he had a complete healing.

The whole story had been invented by his son. The cross he spoke of was a piece of wood which he had picked up in Sydney, Australia, and had had it enclosed in a small silver case. He built up a story about it which fired the imagination of his father, who was very religious. He believed implicitly that he had a piece of the true cross. It was nothing more nor less than blind faith or blind belief.

. . . Go thy way; and as thou hast believed, so be it done unto thee . . . (Matthew 8:13). The father had an instantaneous cure, which took place due to complete acceptance of the magic power of the touch of what he believed to be the true cross. Paracelsus said: "Whether the object of your faith be true or false, you will get the same results."

Do not try to shake other people's beliefs or give them a new philosophy. They are not ready for it. It is their crutch, and if you take away their crutch they fall. Lift them up in your mind and heart and realize that the Healing Light of God flows through them in transcendent loveliness, and the Spirit of Truth leads them to all truth.

Your Aim in Life

If you have a gun and it is cocked, ready to shoot, you can aim it or focus it in whichever direction you choose. You change the direction or angle by changing the base; but when you pull the trigger you have no further control and you cannot control its effect or direction. Likewise, when you are focused, after having placed your attention on a mood of lack or failure and you sleep with that mood, you reproduce it and reap the result. The English language is called the language of angels. An angel is an attitude of mind, a messenger of God. It also means the angle at which you aim. There are numberless angels or attitudes of mind. Therefore, your mood determines whether it is a good aim or a bad aim; a good angel or a bad one.

Discipline your attitude of mind and contemplate what is lovely and of good report. Your camera has a lens. You focus it correctly and you see the object or person clearly; then you take a snapshot. Likewise, your angle or focus must become one with your ideal, which is perfect focusing.

You Name All the Animals

We are told that Adam named all the animals (animated states of consciousness, emotions, moods, feelings). Every man is Adam. You name all the animals. Do you want to feel happy? Do you want to feel sad? Do you want to feel angry, depressed, joyous or resentful? You name all the animals. Every natural fact could be looked upon as a symbol of some spiritual fact. All the appearances in nature correspond to some state of mind. For example, you might say a man in a fit of rage is a lion; a cunning, crafty man is a fox; a man with deep convictions is like a rock; a spiritually minded man is like a torch to others. A lamb symbolizes innocence; a snake is subtle spite; flowers express beauty. When the Bible uses the terms light and darkness, it means knowledge of God and ignorance of truth.

All of us are subject to numberless moods throughout the day. If you go to sleep with the composite moods of the day, you will have certain definite experiences next day unless you neutralize these moods by contemplation of the truths of God prior to sleep. The lower is always subject to the higher, and spiritual truths have the highest vibration. Your moods are brought on by your reactions to the events, experiences and the news of the day.

If a loved one tells you of a terrific disaster and you sympathize with her, you become one with her because you have identified with the morbid, baleful aspects of the situation; therefore, you must express lack. You cannot help her that way. It is not what happens to you; it is your thought about it that matters. You can, therefore, lift the person up in your thoughts by the practice of the Presence of God, or you can sink down in the quicksand with the other.

He sent his word, and healed them . . . (Psalms 107:20).

6

IMAGINATION—THE WORKSHOP OF GOD

Now Israel loved Joseph more than all his children, because he was the son of his old age: and he made him a coat of many colors. And when his brethren saw that their father loved him more than all his brethren, they hated him, and could not speak peaceably unto him. And Joseph dreamed a dream, and he told it his brethren: and they hated him yet the more. And he said unto them, Hear, I pray you, this dream which I have dreamed:

For, behold, we were binding sheaves in the field, and, lo, my sheaf arose, and also stood upright; and, behold, your sheaves stood round about, and made obeisance to my sheaf. And his brethren said to him, Shalt thou indeed reign over us? or shalt thou indeed have dominion over us? And they hated him yet the more for his dreams, and for his words.

And he dreamed yet another dream, and told it his brethren, and said, Behold, I have dreamed a dream more; and, behold, the sun and the moon and the eleven stars made obeisance to me. And he told it to his father, and to his brethren: and his father rebuked him, and said unto him, What is this dream that thou hast dreamed? Shall I and thy mother and thy brethren indeed come to bow down ourselves to thee to the earth? (Genesis 37:3-10).

Joseph in the Bible represents the primal faculty of man; namely, imagination. This faculty has the power to throw onto the screen of visibility in substance and form every idea that the mind may conceive. Joseph is a state of mind in which one increases along all lines—spiritually, mentally, intellectually, financially and professionally. The imagination is the most powerful and productive faculty. Oftentimes it is belittled by the average man, who refers to it as being deceptive and an illusion.

The brethren of Joseph, meaning the other faculties of his mind, deride and scorn Joseph, or imagination, meaning the other faculties, including the five senses, are unawakened spiritually and are functioning at a five-sense level. This is referred to as follows . . . *And they hated him yet the more for his dreams and for his words* (Genesis 37:8).

. . . *Israel loved Joseph more than all his children* . . . (Genesis 37:3). Israel means a prince ruling with God. In other words, it is any man who recognizes the sovereignty of the Spirit within him and who recognizes Spirit (God) as his guide, governing, directing and controlling all his activities. He is under Divine auspices in all his undertakings.

Joseph is the son of his old age. The word son means expression or manifestation. Old age refers to wisdom and understanding of the laws of mind and the way of the Infinite Spirit within man. Old age might be looked upon as not the flight of years, but the dawn of wisdom. Disciplined, controlled, directed imagination is the son of your old age.

Imagination is the mighty instrument used by great scientists, artists, physicists, inventors, architects and mystics. When the world said, "It can't be done; it is impossible," the man with imagination said, "It is done." Through your imagination you can penetrate the depths of reality and reveal the secrets of nature.

Joseph is a dreamer and a dreamer of dreams. This means he has visions, images and ideals in his mind, and he knows there is a Creative Power Which responds to his mental pictures. The mental images we hold are developed in feeling. It is wisely said that all our senses are modifications of the one sense—feeling. Feeling is the fountain head of power. When you delight and rejoice in your mental image, you will automatically generate the appropriate feeling, as every idea has its own fragrance. *Joseph dreamed a dream, and he told it his brethren; and they hated him yet the more* (Genesis 37:5).

Perhaps as you read this you have a dream, an ideal, a plan or purpose that you would like to accomplish. To hate in the Bible is to mentally reject or repudiate that which is false. The thoughts, feelings, beliefs, opinions and judgments in your mind are your brethren, which challenge you, belittle your dream, and say to you: "You can't; it's hopeless; it is impossible; forget it."

For example, you discover there is a quarrel in your own mind with your brethren. Opposition sets in. The way to handle this opposition in your mind is to detach your attention from sense evidence and appearance of things and begin to think clearly and with interest about your goal or objective. When your mind is engaged with your goal or objective, you are using the creative law of mind. Sustain your affirmative attitude of mind and you will experience the joy of the answered prayer.

. . . Lo, my sheaf arose, and also stood upright; and, behold, your sheaves stood round about, and made obeisance to my sheaf (Genesis 37:7). This means that whatever you imagine and feel to be true will come to pass. Lift your ideal up to the point of acceptance in your mind. Exalt it. Commit yourself wholeheartedly to it. Praise your ideal; give your attention, love and devotion to it. And as you continue to do this, knowing that there is only One Power, all the thoughts that deride or scorn your ideal will be neutralized and will make obeisance to your exalted state of mind, i.e., they will lose their power and disappear from the mind.

Through your faculty to imagine the end result, you have control over any circumstance or condition. If you wish to bring about the realization of any wish, desire or idea, form a mental picture of fulfillment in your mind. Constantly imagine the reality of your desire. In this way you will actually compel it into being. What you imagine as true already subsists in the next dimension of mind, and if you remain faithful to your ideal, it will one day objectify itself. The master-architect within you will project on the screen of visibility what you impress on your mind.

Joseph (imagination) wears a coat of many colors. A coat in the Bible represents a garment of the mind; namely, a psychological covering or attitude of mind. Your mental garments are your thoughts, beliefs, moods and expectancy.

The coat of many colors represents the many facets of the diamond, or your capacity to clothe any idea in form. You can imagine your friend, who is poor, living in the lap of luxury. You can see his face light up with joy, see his expression change, and a broad smile cross his lips. You can hear him tell you what you want to hear. You can see him exactly as you wish to see him—i.e., he is radiant, happy, prosperous, and successful. Your imagination is the coat of many colors. It can clothe and objectify any idea or desire. You can imagine abundance where there is lack, peace where there is discord, health where there is sickness, and joy where there is sadness.

And his brethren said to him, Shalt thou indeed reign over us. . . (Genesis 37:8). Imagination is the first faculty, and it takes precedence over all the other powers or elements of consciousness.

And he dreamed yet another dream, and told it his brethren, and said, Behold, I have dreamed a dream more; and, behold, the sun and the moon and the eleven stars made obeisance to me (Genesis 37:9). In ancient symbology, the *sun* and the *moon* represent the conscious and the subconscious mind. The *eleven stars* represent the eleven powers in addition to imagination. Here again, the inspired writer is telling you that disciplined imagination takes precedence over all other faculties of the mind, and it controls the direction of your conscious and subconscious mind. Imagination is first and foremost. It can be scientifically directed.

Joseph in Egypt

This means that what you imagined and felt as true is deposited in your subconscious mind and will come to pass. It represents your highest perception of Truth. In this process, Joseph, or your Divine ideal, seems to die just as a seed dies before it becomes the fruit or the tree. But his "bones" remain. Bones are symbolic of support and symmetry. When your desire is realized, the bones, or the patterns of a new desire, are resurrected in your mind, for you are destined to go from glory to glory. Your journey is ever onward, upward and God-ward.

Shakespeare Used His Imagination

Shakespeare listened to the old stories, fables and myths of his day. In his imagination he clothed all these characters, one by one, with hair, skin, muscle, bone, etc., animating them and making them so much alive in his plays that we think we are reading about ourselves.

Clothe Truth in the Garment of Loveliness and Beauty

With your imaginative eye you could now look at an acorn, and with your imaginative eye construct a magnificent forest full of rivers, rivulets and streams. You could people the forest with all kinds of life.

Furthermore, you could hang a bow on every cloud. You could look at a desert and cause it to rejoice and blossom as the rose. Long hours, hard labor or burning the midnight oil will not produce a Milton, a Shakespeare, a Phidias or a Beethoven. Men accomplish great things through quiet moments, imagining that the invisible things of the Infinite from the foundation of time are clearly visible.

Become a Practical Dreamer

You must put a foundation under your dreams. Decide to make your dreams come true. Withdraw or abstract your attention from the appearance of things. Even though your senses deny what you pray for, affirm it as true in your heart. Bring your mind back from its wandering after the false gods of fear and doubt to rest on the Omnipotence of the Spiritual Presence within you.

In the silence and quietude of your own mind, dwell on the fact that there is only One Power and One Presence. Give all your mental attention to recognizing the absolute sovereignty of the Spiritual Power, knowing that this God-Power has the answer and is now showing you the way. Trust It; believe in It. Walk the earth in the light that your prayer is already answered.

The sculptor looks at a rock. Out of that rock, through Divine imagination, he can reveal the Madonna and portray a vision of beauty and joy forever. The Madonna was in his mind, and he chiseled and chipped away all the parts necessary to reveal the image in his mind.

There Is a Way Out

When the night is black and you see no way out (i.e., when your problem is most acute), let your imagination reveal the solution. *I will lift up mine eyes* (imaginative faculty) *unto the hills, from whence cometh my help* (Psalm 121:1). The hills referred to are of an inner range—the Presence of God within you. When you seek guidance and inspiration, fix your eyes on the stars of God's Truth, such as: "Infinite Intelligence leads and guides me," or "Divine Wisdom reveals to me the answer, and I am inspired from On High."

Man Is the Tabernacle

Every man is the tabernacle of God, and no matter how low he has sunk, the Infinite Healing Presence is there waiting to minister to him. It is within all of us, waiting for us to call upon It. You can use your imagination in all human relationships in a wonderful way.

Imagine yourself to be in the other fellow's place. This tells you what to do. Imagine that the other is expressing all that you long to see him express. See him as he ought to be, not as he appears to be. Perhaps he is surly, sarcastic, bitter, hostile. There may be many frustrated hopes and tragedies lurking in his mind. Salute the Divinity in him; let the Spirit in you talk to the Spirit in him and claim that there are harmony, peace and Divine understanding between you. Surrender him to the Infinite, realizing that the Truths of God are within him, just waiting to be born and released. You can affirm, if you wish, "God waits to be born in him."

It could possibly happen that you may succeed in kindling the fire of God's love in that man's heart, and, perhaps, the spark you lit will burst into a Divine fire.

Let the Masterpiece Come Forth

Leonardo Da Vinci, through his gift of imagination, meditated on the twelve disciples and what they meant. He got lost in deep reverie. His imaginative faculty secreted the perfect pictures from the Infinite Reservoir within him; and due to his perfect focus, his inner eye glowed with an interior luminosity so that he was inspired. Out of his Divine imagery came the masterpiece—The Last Supper.

Imagination Created Your Deck of Cards

Long before our Bible was published, ancient wisdom said, "As a man imagines and feels, so does he become." This ancient teaching is lost in antiquity.

Legend relates that many thousands of years ago, the Chinese sages gathered together under the leadership of the foremost wise man to discuss the fact that vast hordes of brutal invaders were pillaging and plundering the land. The question to be resolved was: How shall we preserve the ancient wisdom from the destruction of the invaders? There were many suggestions. Some thought that the ancient scrolls and symbols should be buried in the Himalayan mountains. Others suggested that the wisdom be deposited in monasteries in Tibet. Still others pointed out that the sacred temples of India were the ideal places for the preservation of the wisdom of God.

The chief sage was silent during the entire discussion; in fact, he went to sleep in the midst of their talk, much to their dismay! He wakened in a little while, however, and said, "Tao (God) gave me the answer, and it is this: We will order the great pictorial artists of China—men gifted with Divine imagination—and tell them what we wish to accomplish. We will initiate them into the mysteries of Truth. They will portray or depict in picture form the eternal verities, which shall be preserved for all time and for countless generations yet unborn.

"When they are finished with the symbolic dramatization of the great truths, powers, qualities and attributes of God through a series of picture cards, we will tell the world about a new game that has been originated. Men throughout the world for all time will use these cards as a game of chance, not knowing that through this simple device, they are preserving the sacred teaching for all generations."

This was probably the origin of the Tarot cards and our present deck of cards, which is derived from them.

The ancient Chinese sage, according to the legend, added, "If all the sacred writings were destroyed, they could again be resurrected at any time through the symbolic teachings and inner meanings of the various designs on the cards."

Imagination clothes all ideas and gives them form. In the act of imagination, that which is hidden in your deeper self is made manifest.

By imagination, what exists in latency, or is asleep within you, is given form in thought. You contemplate that which hitherto had been unrevealed.

You Are Always Using Imagination

Let us take some simple examples: When you were going to get married, you had vivid, realistic pictures in your mind. You imagined you saw the priest, minister or rabbi, and you heard him pronounce the words. You saw the flowers and the church, and you heard the music. You imagined the ring on your finger, and you traveled through your imagination on your honeymoon. All these were mental images created by yourself in your own mind.

Likewise, before graduation, you had a beautiful scenic drama taking place in your mind. You had clothed all your ideas about graduation in form. You imagined the professor or the president of the college giving you your diploma. You saw all the students dressed in gowns.

You heard your mother, father, girl friend or boy friend congratulate you. You felt the embrace and the kiss on your cheek. It was all real, dramatic, exciting and wonderful.

Images appeared freely in your mind as if from nowhere, but you know and must admit there was and is an Internal Creator with the power to mold all these forms which you saw in your mind and endow them with life, motion and voice. These images said to you, "For you only we live!"

Why He Failed Five Times

In a recent conversation with a young man, I discovered the reason why he had failed five times. He had a subconscious picture of failure. Having failed once, he began to say to himself, "I suppose I will fail again." His expectancy and fear brought about his repeated failures. He learned that his subconscious responded according to the nature of his constant imagery; moreover, it took his fear of failure as a request and proceeded to bring it about. He began to realize that his subconscious takes him literally and that it doesn't play jokes on him. He saw he had no will, desire or inclination to succeed.

I explained to him that all he had to do, regardless of his present attitude, was to cast himself in the role of hearing the manager telling him over and over again, "Congratulations on your success. The organization is proud of you." He kept doing this for about 15 minutes every night in a relaxed manner prior to sleep. He would imagine the manager shaking hands with him and using the appropriate words, as mentioned in this paragraph. He kept this up every night until it became natural, reasonable and acceptable to his conscious mind; then, it naturally sank into his subconscious mind. At the end of three weeks promotion suddenly came and he experienced objectively what he had dramatized subjectively.

How the Answer Came

A young medical student, taking his final examination, was presented with a difficult question on *materia medica*. He stilled his mind, relaxed a few minutes, and said over and over again slowly, "Infinite Intelligence knows the answer and reveals it to me." In the meantime, he went on answering the other questions, which were easy. In a short while the picture of the answer came clearly into his mind. It appeared in words like the page of a book, with the entire answer written out as a graph in the mind. He had relaxed his conscious mind; then the subjective wisdom gave him the answer, which came clearly into his conscious, reasoning mind.

Is Your Premise Correct?

Your mind works like a syllogism. If your premise is correct, the conclusion or result will correspond. Your subconscious mind reasons deductively only, and its sequence or conclusion is always in harmony with the premise. Establish the right premise in your mind and you will be subjectively compelled to right action. Your external movements and actions are the automatic response of the internal motion of your mind. Hearing a friend or associate congratulate you over and over again on your wonderful decision will induce the movement of right action in your life.

How Goethe Used His Imagination

Goethe used his imagination wisely when confronted with difficulties and predicaments. His biographers point out that he was accustomed to fill many hours quietly holding imaginary conversations. It is well known that his custom was to imagine one of his friends before him in a chair answering in the right way. In other words, if he were concerned over any problem, he imagined that his friend was giving him the right or appropriate answer, accompanied with the usual gestures, tonal qualities of the voice, and making the entire imaginary scene as real and vivid as possible.

How He Solved Financial Problems

A stock broker who used to attend my lectures in Steinway Hall, New York City, many years ago revealed to me his method of solving financial difficulties, which was extraordinarily simple. He would have mental, imaginary conversations with a multi-millionaire banker friend of his, who congratulated him over and over again on his wise and sound judgments regarding investments and who would compliment him on his purchase of the right stocks. He used to dramatize this imaginary conversation until he had psychologically fixed it as a form of belief in his mind, and his subconscious mind responded, resulting in his being an outstanding success.

Mr. Nicoll, a student of Ouspensky, used to say, "Watch your inner talking and let it agree with your aim."

This broker's inner talking or speech certainly agreed with his aim to make sound investments for himself and his clients. He told me his main purpose in his business life was to make money for others and to see them prosper financially by his wise counsel. It is quite obvious he was using the laws of mind constructively.

It is the sustained mental picture which is developed in the dark house of the mind. Run your mental movie often. Get into the habit of flashing it on the screen of your mind frequently. After a while it will become a definite mental pattern. The inner movie which you have seen with your mind's eye shall be made manifest openly.

. . . *And calleth those things which be not as though they were* (Romans 4:17).

7

Spiritual Gems of Truth

I am the vine, ye are the branches . . . (John 15:5). Whatever you attach to I AM, you magnify. I AM magnifies every state of mind. For example, if you say, "I am poor, I am lonesome, I am miserable," you magnify those mental conditions. It is like the number 9, because 9 added to any number does not alter it. On the contrary, it magnifies the number; e.g., supposing you add 9 to 5. You have 14, but 4 + 1 = 5.

The I AM within you, which means Being, Life, Awareness, Self-Originating Spirit, etc. is God, or the Life-Principle. I AM is the true Christmas tree, and all gifts are on the Christmas tree, for God is both the giver and the gift. If you work for someone and he pays you, he is liquidating an obligation; but I AM is a gift to you. No work or sacrifice is needed.

Peace is now. The God of peace is within you and you can claim it. Love is now. Open your mind and heart to the influx of Divine love now, for God is the Eternal Now! Power is now, poise is now and joy is now. The Healing Presence is within you, and you can claim that the Infinite Healing Presence is flowing through you now, this very minute. The answer to your problem, whatever it is, is within you now, for Infinite Intelligence knows all things.

. . . Before they call, I will answer . . . (Isaiah 65:24). God is timeless, spaceless and ageless. Take your good now. You might as well claim all your good now as to do so a hundred years from now. Why wait?

Your Imagination and Will

If you put a six foot plank on the floor, you can walk the length of it without any hesitancy, but if the plank is placed thirty feet high in the air between two homes and you are asked to walk on it, you might develop some qualms, for when you look down and your imagination tells you there is no solid foundation, you become afraid and your imagination, therefore, wins. When you try to will something into being by mental coercion or will power, you are using the law of reverse action, because it is as though you are saying, "I will be well, I will be strong, I will be wealthy," when actually what you are saying is, "I am sick, I am weak, I am poor." . . . *Let the weak say, I am strong* (Joel 3:10).

Your subconscious is like a recording machine, and it records what you decree. *Greater love hath no man than this, that a man lay down his life for his friends* (John 15:13). Your friend is that which befriends you; therefore, you give up the old state and focus your attention on your ideal, thereby giving life to it. By getting into the mood and tonal quality and living in the reality of it, you will die to the old state and live to the new.

You must realize that the idea you have in your mind is real. It is a psychological fact. But to make it concrete or tangible, or make it appear in my world, I must sense it or get into the mood which is creative, and then walk in the light and realization that it will come to pass.

If your attitude of mind is: "Well, I might get it. I'll try, but I know it is impossible. Maybe some future time," these are moods or feelings and they will be expressed inevitably as disappointments, frustration and unrealized hopes . . . *This day is this scripture fulfilled in your ears* (Luke 4:21).

Remember, all of us are between two thieves—the past and the future. Nothing is accomplished by looking at either one. Many dwell on old hurts, peeves, grudges and losses of years ago. Others are full of fear regarding the future. They are afraid of old age, sickness, insecurity and death. All the good you seek is now, for God is the Eternal Now! All the attributes, qualities and potencies of God are instantly available to you. The Spirit within you is timeless, spaceless and ageless.

The Wonders of the Mind

On a recent visit to Ireland and England, I talked with an English niece. She told me that on a recent visit she had made to Killarney, she felt she had been there before. She knew her way around the place, and said she knew what people would say to her before she asked questions. Many of the shops and even their contents were known to her.

The answer I gave her was very simple. Many people have the same experience in visiting foreign cities and countries. It is not due to a previous incarnation, however. She had made careful plans for the trip, she purchased a ticket to fly to Ireland, visualized a wonderful time, impressed her subconscious and went to sleep on it. Her subconscious knows all and sees all, and she traveled there psychologically and dwelt there subjectively for a while, then when her conscious mind arrived there, she heard the voices based on former impressions, which she may have forgotten. But when she heard the voices, it was the objectification of her psychological journey, and it registered.

How to Practice the Presence of God

Calmly trust God's Holy Presence to lead you to green pastures and to still waters. Love the Truth with a love that leaves no room for care or doubt. No matter what your work may be, as you go to your business, say, "God walks and talks in me. I completely rely on God's guidance and wisdom." Give thanks for the perfect day. Do as Brother Lawrence suggests: Whenever your attention wanders away onto fear or doubt, bring it back to the contemplation of His Holy Presence.

To secure and to know the life of peace and joy, school yourself daily to have an intimate, loving, familiar, humble conversation with God—all day long. Let wonders happen in your life.

Your Assumptions Become Facts

During a recent conversation with an English army officer, he pointed out that Adolph Hitler, at the time of the armistice at the close of the First World War, was a prisoner. He refused to accept the fact that Germany was beaten, however. He went blind for a period of six weeks or longer, but it was a psychological blindness—no organic reason could be found.

In the dark silence in which he existed he embodied the ideal of the German people at that time, which was a desire for vengeance or to get even, because of the wrongs they felt had been inflicted on them due to the Versailles Treaty. His assumption of that attitude made an impression on his subconscious mind, which responded accordingly. His name was Schickelgruber while a prisoner. When released, he be- came Hitler, and he no longer responded to Schickelgruber. He awoke a different man, having a new concept of himself.

You also can use your subconscious for good or ill. It is all things to all men. Assume that you are illumined, noble and Godlike. As you keep up that attitude of mind, it will gel within you and your assumption will crystallize into a fact . . . *When deep sleep falleth upon men, in slumberings upon the bed; then he openeth the ears of men, and sealeth their instruction* (Job 33:15-16). Oftentimes man is instructed what to do during sleep time. For example, suppose you are seeking an answer to a perplexing problem. You could say to your deeper mind prior to sleep: "I seek an answer or solution to this problem." Then condense the sentence down to one word, "Answer," and repeat it slowly. In other words, lull yourself to sleep with one word, "Answer," and you will receive the solution either in a dream, vision of the night, or as a flash of illumination as you awaken in the morning.

It is said that the Russian General Cynarsky during the Napoleonic Wars paid no attention to the advice of his associates on the General Staff, who were mapping strategy. He went to sleep contemplating only one thing—victory. He saw the end and snored while his associates discussed plans. He had his plan, and impregnated his subconscious mind with the idea of victory. He did not want to be swayed. Cynarsky undoubtedly knew that the conscious mind is inductive, i.e., it reasons from a premise such as 2 + 2 = 4, and it deduces the results from this. It bases its findings on factual evidence and reason, regarding the future or the probable. The subconscious mind is deductive only. It takes all impressions given it as facts. It is wholly impersonal. It accepts the idea as existing now and acts accordingly. His conviction of victory impressed his subconscious mind and consequently it came to pass.

Your conscious mind is sometimes called the father; the subconscious the mother.

Upon this I awaked, and beheld; and my sleep was sweet unto me (Jeremiah 31:26).

A young woman with a wonderful voice tried to get a position singing on the radio or television but failed. She tried too hard and was overly anxious, tense and worried, which blocked her good. At my suggestion, prior to sleep she began to relax her entire body by closing her eyes and talking to herself this way: "My feet are relaxed, my ankles are relaxed, my toes are relaxed, the calves of my legs are relaxed, my abdominal muscles are relaxed, my heart and lungs are relaxed, my spine is relaxed, my neck is relaxed, my hands and arms are relaxed, my brain is relaxed, my face is relaxed. I am completely relaxed and at peace."

She repeated these suggestions four or five times, while knowing that the body had to obey her. She said, "I felt very sleepy, completely relaxed and non-resistant. I heard the clock tick, the baby snoring, but I had no desire to move or do anything. In that sleepy state I affirmed: 'I am a singer on TV now. It is wonderful!' Having framed the sentence, I shortened it to one word, 'TV,' knowing that my subconscious knows all. I repeated 'TV over and over again arid lulled myself to sleep with the one word, TV.' The next morning my agent called me, saying he had a spot for me. My prayer was answered."

The above illustration is a very simple way of conveying the idea or desire of your heart to your subconscious mind.

She Had a Recurrent Dream of a Loved One Having Died

One of our radio listeners wrote me, saying she had dreamed seven or eight times of a loved one dying, someone whom she cared for and who was very close to her. But she added that the person is very much alive. I explained to her that if she dreams of a person she loves as having died, it doesn't necessarily mean that the loved one will die or has died, but it means that something she loves in her life, such as position, quality or health, is dying or has died—not the person.

Actually, her love for her husband had died, as she knew he had a mistress. Her love had turned to hate, and her subconscious was reminding her. This hate within her was murdering love, peace, harmony and joy and was beginning to affect her body in the form of arthritis.

Accordingly, she talked the matter over with her husband and they arranged for an amicable divorce. As she began to appraise herself spiritually, realizing she was a daughter of the Infinite and a child of Eternity, she ceased hating and instead built up self-esteem, while realizing that her true Self was God. Her constant prayer was, "God loves me and cares for me. His peace fills my soul. God's love saturates my whole being, and the light of God illumines my pathway." When thoughts of her ex-husband came to her mind, she affirmed immediately, "God loves me and cares for me."

After awhile all anger, resentment and hatred was dissolved in the light of God's love. She said, "I stopped trying to force myself to bless him. I knew that as I saturated my mind and heart with Divine love, all the negatives would disappear, which they did." There was no longer any sting in her mind. Her hatred and rage were suppressed in her subconscious, and being of a very destructive nature, had to have a negative outlet, which was appearing as arthritis. The suppleness and mobility of her knees have been restored, as love dissolves everything unlike itself.

An interesting sequel to her prayer process was that she had a tremendous urge to finish the study of medicine, having previously completed two years in medical college in New York. She is now well on the way to becoming a pediatrician and, undoubtedly, she will be a wonderful doctor.

If you dream of a person you dislike very much as dead or dying, it means that the condition or thing in your life embodied or symbolized by that person has died or passed away. To illustrate this point, a young college girl dreamed that her ex-fiancé was dead. This dream occurred during three consecutive nights. However, he was very much alive.

Her doctor had diagnosed a tumor in her creative organ. She realized the relationship and said to me, "I know the growth is one of resentment, but I have been going to Unity Church and Science of Mind classes, and I know it will pass away." I suggested to her that as far as I could judge, the tumor undoubtedly was dissolved. I pointed out to her the significance of her dream and suggested that she go to her gynecologist for another examination. She did, and he confirmed the truth of her dream. Her subconscious, speaking to her symbolically, told her that all her resentment and hostility had died in her, and that the physical embodiment of her negative emotions had disappeared also.

. . . Who will shew us any good? Lord, lift thou up the light of thy countenance upon us. Thou hast put gladness in my heart. . . I will both lay me down in peace, and sleep: for thou, Lord, only makest me dwell in safety (Psalm 4:6-8). *Yea, they turned back and tempted God, and limited the*

Holy One of Israel. They remembered not his hand, nor the day when he delivered them from the enemy (Psalm 78:41-42).

You must never limit the Infinite. It is Omnipotent and Omniscient. The hand means the power of God, and the enemies are of our own mind, such as fear, doubt, jealousy, etc. Divine love casts out all fear, and you are delivered from the limitations which you have placed upon yourself. When faced with a problem, challenge or difficult assignment, look at it and say to yourself that the problem is here but God is here also. The problem, sickness, disease or whatever is then immediately Divinely outmatched. Don't turn your back on the Infinite Presence and Power within you. When you call upon the Presence, you will get an answer, for Its nature is responsiveness.

His Dissatisfaction Led to Satisfaction

A young engineer attending one of my classes on the inner meaning of the Bible said to me that all his life he had been irritated and upset with the religious beliefs communicated to him by his parents and teachers in his church. I explained to him that irritation causes oysters to give birth to pearls. His irritation caused him to delve into the religions of the world and to discover the inner meaning of the parables, allegories and fables. He is now studying *The Power of Your Subconscious Mind* and applying the techniques outlined therein.

It is true that irritation with your religious beliefs or your limitations, such as a faulty or unhappy marriage, causes you to seek truth or freedom. If you are supremely happy along religious, political and social lines, you don't seek truth. It is because certain things went wrong that you sought a greater answer and a way out. Then your subjective self opened a new door for you, and a new light or spiritual awareness was born. When you look back upon the irritation or the problem, you should be grateful and thankful for the challenge, and praise and bless the experience.

Before Abraham Was, I Am (John 8:58)

Before any manifestation appears on the screen of space, it comes from the Invisible. All of us came forth from the Living Spirit Almighty. Before you appeared on this plane, you were Spirit. When coition takes place between the father and mother, the tone or mood captured at that moment brings into being out of Itself a child in harmony with the note struck. It is like a piano: You strike a note and all notes in harmony vibrate. If you are playing a perfect chord and strike a dissonance, or if you are playing a beautiful piece of music and strike a note not in harmony with same, it will bring out a dissonance or discord.

This applies also to a misshapen child. If you are drunk and have coition, or are under the influence of narcotics, a distorted or malformed child could come forth. The infinite keyboard of the Infinite is within us, and we can strike any tone we wish. If the dominant mood or tone during coition is, "I hate to hear that voice," or "I hate the sight of —," in that mood, if the ovum is fertilized, a deaf or blind child could be born. Likewise, if the parents could get into the mood of Mozart, they could possibly create another Mozart who could play at three years of age.

Each person is a movement of Infinity on the screen of space. You gravitate to your parents according to the tone or mood of parents at the moment of conception. In other words, you are the Infinite Spirit appearing as a child in the home of your parents. Quimby said it correctly when he said, "You are a Spirit now. You were always a Spirit. When will you cease to be a Spirit?" You are conditioned as John Jones to believe yourself to be a man, age—, carpenter, American, etc. Actually, you are I AM (God) appearing in the form of man of a certain age, race and profession. It is the One Being appearing as many. Mozart's father didn't have to know music. The I AM within you produces anything and everything.

But of that day and hour knoweth no man, no, not the angels of heaven, but my Father only (Matthew 24:36). Seeds mature at different periods according to their kind. Likewise, seeds or impressions mature in your mind at different periods—months, days or years. No man knows. The reason something turns up which you do not expect is this: Perhaps many years ago you were in business and you had a partner who embezzled money and caused bankruptcy. When you think of it now and get excited or angry, you are living the role over again, as the roots are not withered. It's not forgotten. The proof that you have eradicated the hurt and forgiven yourself for harboring destructive thoughts is that you can remember it and remain indifferent. You have no feeling or sting left.

If you live the scene over again, you create it in your mind; and like the seed that recedes and grows again, quarterly, annually, biannually, e.g., certain plants die and bud again according to the season, in the same way your old condition in a new form appears and you wonder where it came from. To prove to yourself that you are free, sincerely try to see the other person as happy, harmonious, joyous and free. If you cannot do this, you have not forgiven or forsaken. These are the weeds you must pluck out. The roots are there.

Roots are withered by indifference. If you want to kill the roots of resentment within you, listen to the voice of that person telling you what a beautiful, dignified person you are, how honest and kind you are. Make it real. You want to hear it. Get into the mood. It works. This is a technique used by many. Another technique is to affirm as follows: "I release—to the Infinite and wish for him all the blessings of life. Any time he comes to my mind I will immediately affirm, 'I have released you. God be with you." As you keep this up, the moment comes when he comes to your mind and there is no longer any sting. The roots of resentment and anger are withered, and you are at peace.

She Got the Wrong Advice

During an interview with a woman who had a marital problem, she said that the counselor had told her to let loose her expressions of temper and rage on her husband, whom she hated. As a result, they had been pouring out venom on each other. These mental poisons were polluting her mind and body. I explained to her that such advice as she received is stupid and destructive. It is foolish and idiotic to think that the way to get rid of a destructive emotion is to express it.

If this happened to be true, the opposite would have to be true. I asked her if she expressed love, cordiality and geniality, would she get rid of love that way? Of course not. Her subconscious would magnify love and goodwill. God is love, and His love indwells all people. Begin to exude vibrancy and goodwill to all those around you, and you will magnify and reinforce these qualities in your mind and heart.

This woman did not eradicate or expunge hatred and hostility from her subconscious by expressing it; she was getting worse by the hour. The two were living a lie, and it takes two to make a 'go' of marriage. A harmonious reconciliation can only take place on a spiritual basis. There is a principle of right action and no principle of wrong action. The right thoughts, the right mood and right action bring about a balanced mind. There is no penalty in love or right action.

Both of them decided to preserve the marriage and began to alternate in prayer each night. She would read the 23rd Psalm out loud one night and he would read the 91st Psalm the next night. Each one came to a decision to exalt God in each other. When he was ready to explode, he would immediately supplant the negative thoughts with: "God loves her and cares for her. I exalt God in the midst of her." Repetition of this prayer became a habit for both of them. She decided to use the same technique: "God loves him and cares for him. I exalt God in the midst of him." The marriage is growing more blessed as the days roll by.

8

Speaking in Other Tongues

> *And when the day of Pentecost was fully come, they were all with one accord in one place. And suddenly there came a sound from heaven as of a rushing mighty wind, and it filled all the house where they were sitting. And there appeared unto them cloven tongues like as of fire, and it sat upon each of them. And they were all filled with the Holy Ghost, and began to speak with other tongues, as the Spirit gave them utterance* (Acts 2:1-4).

The "Day of Pentecost" was with the Israelites the great feast of the harvest. The real inner meaning of the "Day of Pentecost," however, is that as you meditate and give attention to the eternal verities, you begin to give expression to them and they become living realities in your life instead of theoretical concepts held by your conscious mind. In other words, you reap the fruit of the spiritual truths you have been meditating on, and you have entered into the light or illumined reason referred to as the promised land in the Bible. You are living in the promised land when you are expressing harmony, health, peace, joy and abundance.

You gather your thoughts, feelings and mental images together and focus on one thing: The Living Spirit within you. In other words, you turn within and contemplate God within you as boundless love, infinite intelligence, absolute harmony, omnipotent and omniscient. Your thoughts and ideas are now with one accord in one place, and your place is always with God.

They were all with one accord in one place, means the concentrated or focused attention of all the faculties and activities of mind in exaltation and praise of the Infinite Spirit within.

In verse 2, the sound from heaven and the mighty wind represent the movement of the Spirit through our minds and hearts, and the sound from heaven is the joy of the answered prayer.

When you make a habit of prayer and communing with the Infinite, you find the exhilaration of the Spirit animating, inspiring and sustaining you, which is symbolic of the stimulating effect of new wine . . . *These men are full of new wine* (Acts 2:13).

The ultimate result of this transfusion of the Spirit throughout your entire being is that you are definitely inspired to express Truth in a new way—with enthusiasm, fervor and joy. This is called speaking with other tongues.

The cloven tongues of fire spoken of represent the illumination and inspiration following your veneration and adoration of the Infinite Presence and Power within you.

And how hear we every man in our own tongue, wherein we were born? (Acts 2:8). The universal language or tongue is love. All men feel it, understand it and recognize it.

Literally speaking, you can hypnotize a person and suggest to him that he is now speaking in other languages, and you will hear a lot of gibberish. Sometimes in a trance state a medium will speak in different languages because the subjective mind knows all languages, as these are recorded on the Akashic record (the universal or collective unconscious). Speaking in a hypnotic trance in other languages is no indication of spirituality or illumination. Glossolalia, or gift of tongues, may be easily produced in the hypnotic trance. It is merely a feat of subjective memory and is no indication of spiritual enlightenment.

Sir William Hamilton, in his *Lectures on Metaphysics*, Page 148, designates the phenomenon as "latent memory." He says: ". . . For example, there are cases in which the extinct memory of whole languages was suddenly restored, and what is still more remarkable, in which the faculty was exhibited of accurately repeating, in known or unknown tongues, passages which were never within the grasp of conscious memory in the normal strain."

Mr. Coleridge, in his *Biographia Literaria*, cites a case which I am condensing to a brief narrative, as there are countless such cases happening all the time. He says: A young woman about 25 who could neither read nor write was seized with a fever and continued incessantly talking Latin, Greek, and Hebrew, in very pompous tones, and with most distinct enunciation. A physician did some research work and found that this woman had been charitably taken care of by an old Protestant pastor. It appeared that it had been the old man's custom to walk up and down in his house and to read out loud from Rabbinical writings, together with those of several of the Greek and Latin fathers, and the research doctor identified passages taken down at her bedside with passages in the various books.

It is easy to understand the origin of this woman's speaking in other tongues or strange languages. As a child she heard the pastor reciting these passages, and when her conscious mind was in abeyance or subjugated due to fever or other abnormal state, her subconscious memory was released. She reproduced what she had heard. The record upon the tablet of her subconscious mind was ineffaceable.

Thousands of similar cases are recorded, and in this light, the feats of trance speakers are easily explicable without invoking the aid of disembodied spirits. Remember, all languages are inscribed indelibly in your subconscious mind, and so is a memory of everything that has ever transpired since the dawn of time.

You must see the inner meaning behind every story in the Bible. For instance, a man is in the hospital and is in pain, suffering from some disease. He is complaining or bemoaning his fate. He is speaking in the tongues of sickness. When he is healed, however, whether through prayer or the ministrations of a physician, he now speaks in a new tongue—and the new language is the joy of health, vitality and peace of mind. The new tongue spoken of in the Bible is the new mood of understanding which man possesses.

Tongue (Biblically) means mood, tone, vibration or feeling. The universal tongue is love, for "God is love." All men sense the mood of love. Resentment, hate, jealousy, ill will and hostility are foreign tongues, while the gentle, loving smile is understood by all. This universal language or tongue of love has neither height nor depth, length nor breadth; it fills all space. It is the universal solvent and healing balm.

The disciples are your disciplined faculties of mind, and you have twelve faculties. In prayer you gather all your faculties together and withdraw from the objective world and the evidence of the senses and tune in with the Infinite Healing Presence within you. There you dwell on your ideal or the solution to your problem. In this quiet, passive, receptive state, claim that the Almighty Power and wisdom of the Infinite is now flowing through you. Feel the movement of the Spirit through you. In the same way you feel the warmth of the sun. This peaceful, confident mood is the mighty wind or Spirit of God which fills your mind.

The cloven tongues of fire descend upon you. *For our God is a consuming fire* (Hebrews 12:29). The old state is consumed and the new state is born. Your consuming wish of having heard the good news or the joy of the answered prayer burns up the old state and gives birth to the new. The fires of illumination and inspiration have touched every one of your faculties and you are spiritually enriched.

A word fitly spoken is like apples of gold in pictures of silver (Proverbs 25:11). Our words should radiate peace, love, and harmony to all. In other words, we should affirm boldly that the Infinite Spirit thinks, speaks and acts through us and that all those listening to us are lifted up and inspired and miraculously made whole. Your hearers will be subjectively aware of an indefinable essence permeating your words, for when you exude vibrancy and light and love to all, it is called the perfume of the gods.

. . . *The multitude came together, and were confounded, because that every man heard them speak in his own language* (Acts 2:6). The multitude of thoughts in your conscious, reasoning, argumentative mind does not understand what is taking place, as the ways of the Infinite are not the ways of man. *For the wisdom of this world is foolishness with God* . . . (I Corinthians 3:19).

When your prayer is answered, you have heard in your own tongue. Your belief brought it to pass. The wine of life is the new interpretation of life, which transforms you from the waters of life—the dull, insipid, dreary side of life—into the joy of living and expressing more of your innate Divinity.

Peter said: *For these are not drunken, as ye suppose, seeing it is but the third hour of the day* (Acts 2:15). Peter means unshakeable faith in God—the One Power. Peter portrays the quality of absolute conviction that God answers our prayers. In the phrase "the third hour of the day," the latter word "day" indicates light or truth, and the "third hour" is always the inner feeling or awareness that a subjective embodiment of our desire has taken place.

The late Dr. Alexis Carrel, Nobel Prize winner and author of *Man, the Unknown*, points out the marvelous effects produced by prayer. He cites the instance of a cancerous sore which shriveled to a scar in front of his eyes. In addition, he has observed wounds and lesions heal in a few seconds, and others in a few hours with all pathological symptoms disappearing. Through prayer, extreme activation of the processes of organic repair sets in. These healings of body growths, tumors, and burns are due to nothing more than the descent of the tongues of fire mentioned in this chapter.

God is the only healing process. When you tune in to this Infinite Healing Power with faith and expectancy, plus a fired imagination, the influx of the Spirit will respond, permeating your whole being and restoring you to wholeness. The electronic structure of your body is transformed in accordance with the Pattern on the Mount—harmony, wholeness and perfection.

You Are the Captain on the Bridge

The Divine Presence is within you. Sometimes it is called the Primal Energy. Energy is a term used by science for Spirit, or God. It devolves on each of us how we use this Energy. You can use intellectual energy to study or ponder, physical energy to walk, emotional energy to get angry, become resentful or fret and fuss, all of which is destructive to the tissues and your physical organism. You can also use the force of energy to kill or injure, which is very negative.

Take electricity: It is a force; you can use it to light the house, give illumination, or turn on the fan. Motor energy can be used to heat the house by turning on the electric heater or turn on the radio for voice and music. There are different kinds of energy: light, heat and motor energy. You must determine how you are going to use Spiritual energy for your own upliftment and spiritual benefit. Some men spend most of their time eating and drinking, and it shows on their bodies. Others devote all their attention to whiskey and sensuality, which is destructive and clouds the spiritual part of man. Still others get into fits of temper, which ruin their health, bringing on illness and premature death. Others follow the horses, and a good look at them immediately tells you that they have been following the noble steed.

The student is also known. The farmer looks different from the lawyer and the doctor. All are good and honorable, but it merely shows where their attention has been placed. This is marked and portrayed on the physical body. All the basic fundamental truths of man are simple. The erroneous concepts are complicated, confused, and difficult to grasp. Think of the Infinite Presence and Power when you have a problem. Dwell on the solution. Do not get tense. The answer will come in Divine order.

Your conscious mind could be likened to the captain on the bridge. He directs the engineers in the engine room. The captain doesn't steer the ship; he issues orders. If these orders are wrong, the men in the engine room might, for example, hit an iceberg for all they know. The captain might order full speed ahead or astern, and the order is carried out. You are constantly giving mental orders to your subconscious mind. If your decrees are not based on universal principles and eternal verities, you will create chaos in your life.

Enthrone Divine ideas in your conscious mind, mothered by Divine love. This is the government of the free. As you focus your mind directly on the eternal truths of life, you will begin to speak in a new tongue, which will be a mellifluous and melodious voice of wisdom, truth, beauty, joy and goodwill to all. *Your words will be . . . sweet to the soul and health to the bones* (Proverbs 16:24). The word "fire" is an ancient term for God, or Spirit. Energy is a scientific term for Spirit, or God.

There Is an Answer to Every Problem

And Jacob was left alone; and there wrestled a man with him until the breaking of the day. And when he saw that he prevailed not against him, he touched the hollow of his thigh; and the hollow of Jacob's thigh was out of joint, as he wrestled with him. And he said, Let me go, for the day breaketh. And he said, I will not let thee go, except thou bless me. And he said unto him, What is thy name? And he said, Jacob. And he said, Thy name shall be called no more Jacob, but Israel: for as a prince hast thou power with God and with men, and hast prevailed. And Jacob asked him, and said, Tell me, I pray thee, thy name. And he said, Wherefore is it that thou dost ask after my name? And he blessed him there. And Jacob called the name of the place Penuel: for I have seen God face to face, and my life is preserved. And as he passed over Penuel the sun rose upon him, and he halted upon his thigh. Therefore the children of Israel eat not of the sinew which shrank, which is upon the hollow of the thigh, unto this day: because he touched the hollow of Jacob's thigh in the sinew that shrank (Genesis 32:24-32).

Jacob means man awaking to the Presence and Power of God within him. The word "thigh" is a euphemistic expression representing the creative organs of man. The significance of the changing of Jacob's name to Israel is this: Israel means a man who sees God or a prince ruling with God, all of which means he now comprehends that the I AM within him is God—the only Presence and Power—and he gives no allegiance to any other power. He is controlled by Infinite Spirit, which thinks, speaks and acts through him. A great light of understanding indwells the mind, and the type of mind which feels the Presence of God within him is called Israel.

Jacob means you yourself wrestling with a problem in your mind until the breaking of the day. At daylight the sun comes up and the dawn appears. Nighttime is the playground of your subconscious where the subjective powers begin to function and answers come sometimes in dreams and visions of the night.

Prior to sleep look at your problem, try to solve it, study it from all angles, then take your attention away from it, knowing that Infinite Intelligence in your subconscious knows the answer and will reveal it to you. Turn your request over to your deeper mind, which is full of wisdom and understanding, as follows: "I am surrendering this request to my subjective mind, knowing the answer will be revealed to me in Divine order. I sleep in peace and I wake in joy." Oftentimes, when you awaken, the first thought you have is the answer. If not, repeat the request the next night as if you had never done it before. The answer will come to you in Divine order.

How She Got the Answer

A woman once told me how she had wrestled with a problem. She had been accused falsely by two relatives of influencing her aunt to change her Will prior to the latter's demise. There was no truth in the allegation of these relatives, however, but they swore out false affidavits, causing her great anguish and embarrassment. Her attorney was a spiritually oriented man, and he helped her considerably in the litigation.

At my suggestion, she quieted her mind and affirmed: "Infinite Spirit is all wise, and I now decree that the Infinite law of justice, truth, love and harmony is operating perfectly in me, through my attorney and all concerned. The law of harmony and right action prevails. I decree this, and any time the problem comes to my mind, I will affirm immediately, 'God is taking care of that.'"

Following this procedure, a great sense of peace came over her, and she had no further desire to pray about it. Her decree gestated in the darkness of her subconscious mind, and at the end of a week the full- blown answer was presented to her. This, in Bible language, was the breaking of the day. The two relatives contesting the Will suddenly dropped the case altogether and disappeared from sight.

The Bible says, . . . *He touched the hollow of his thigh; and the hollow of Jacob's thigh was out of joint, as he wrestled with him.* The word "thigh," as previously mentioned, is a phallic symbol. The Bible is full of phallic symbols which reveal profound psychological and spiritual truths. After the copulative act, man's creative organs shrink, and he is relaxed. Some religious groups will not eat of the area of the animal which is related to the area of Jacob's thigh. This, of course, is not the meaning of it, and it makes no sense.

During the meditative act as portrayed by the woman above with the legal problem, she felt a great sense of peace following the prayer technique. She was relaxed and at ease and knew intuitively that the problem was solved. In Bible language, the sinew shrank, which meant that her mental work was finished.

While visiting some time ago in Cork City, Ireland, I learned that a relative of mine had lost her voice. Doctors could find nothing wrong with her and believed it to be emotional. I explained to her that she becomes what she contemplates. Accordingly, she began to sit quietly several times a day and imagined she was singing gloriously and majestically before an imaginary audience. In her mind's eye, she saw and heard the audience applaud her. Gradually, she began to feel the reality and wonder of it all, and at the end of the third day, suddenly something went out of her; or, in Bible language, *Somebody hath touched me: for I perceive that virtue* (the healing power of God) *is gone out of me* (Luke 8:46).

Her voice was restored. She experienced a successful meditation and was incapable of continuing the meditative act. After praying successfully, you are as relaxed as after the physical creative act. When satisfaction is yours, you no longer hunger for it. If the desire persists, you did not succeed in impregnating your subconscious mind. In other words, you did not succeed in becoming aware of being what you had wanted to be.

When your prayer is answered, something definitely shrinks within you; not in a physical standpoint, but in your subjective feeling nature. You lose all desire to continue in your particular meditation. When you pray successfully and believe in your heart that you are already that which you desire to be, at that moment of satisfaction something goes out of you physically and psychologically, which testifies to your creative power.

In Genesis 32:31, it says: *And as he passed over Penuel the sun rose upon him, and he halted upon his thigh.* Penuel or Peniel means the inner realization of the Divine Presence and of having succeeded through prayer in attaining the Divine favor and blessing sought. The word "halted" means you are now at peace, as your prayer is answered.

Therefore I say unto you, What things soever ye desire, when ye pray, believe that ye receive them, and ye shall have them (Mark 11:24).

9

Learn to Let Go in Life

Agree with thine adversary quickly, whitest thou art in the way with him; lest at any time the adversary deliver thee to the judge, and the judge deliver thee to the officer, and thou be cast into prison. Verily I say unto thee, Thou shall by no means come out thence, till thou hast paid the uttermost farthing (Matthew 5:25-26).

The above Biblical verses do not mean that you should agree with that which is false or that which instills fear into your mind. To agree means to harmonize, and when you tune in with the Infinite Presence and Power within you and claim that what is true of the Infinite is true of you, then you are in agreement with the eternal verities and you mentally reject anything and everything that does not lift you up, inspire, heal, bless and restore your soul.

How She Agreed

A young girl who had been studying the Science of Mind recently went on vacation to her old home in Iowa. Her father criticized her new belief about God, life and the universe. He was vehement in his denunciation of her rejection of hell, damnation, lost souls, etc. She came to terms with his belief, however, and she reached a definite conclusion in her mind, saying to her father, "Dad, you are free to believe whatever you like, such as hell, the devil, lake of fire, etc.; but I positively, definitely and absolutely reject all such beliefs.

You are free to adhere to such concepts, and I am free to believe the way I do. I still love you and wish for you all the blessings of life."

They then came to an understanding and respected each other's beliefs. She came to a decision in her mind and refused to be disturbed by her father's illogical beliefs. If she had resented her father's outburst and had become incensed and angry, she would have been delivered to the judge, which simply means the judgment or decision in her own mind. Her judgment or thought of her father would be her own thought about herself. Since thought is creative, she would be generating mental poisons in her own blood stream. Then, as the Bible says, she would be cast into prison—the prison of sickness, fear and negative emotions, which would rob her of vitality, enthusiasm and energy. She knew that the adversary was in her own mind, and she cast it out.

She Learned to Agree with Her Attorney

A few months ago I recommended to a woman that she seek the services of a criminal attorney. I suggested a spiritually oriented lawyer. She went to see him and was very happy with his advice and handling of the case. One day, however, she called me up, telling me she was furious at this attorney. Upon being asked why, she said that she had gone into a restaurant after the court hearing and had seen him having lunch with the opposing attorney, who had been terribly nasty and ugly to her in his cross examination. She added, "I can't understand why you recommended him."

I explained to her a simple truth. I told her by way of example how I had engaged in a vigorous debate with Dr. Ernest Wilson, head of the Unity Church in Kansas City, Missouri, where we contradicted each other on the subject of reincarnation. Yet, we are the best of friends and laugh and joke about our differences on the subject of reincarnation. He has written a book on all the reasons why it is so, and I have written a chapter in *Psychic Perception:*

The Magic of Extrasensory Power on why it is not so. We may differ on the subject, but we have sense enough to know that at the same time we can be amiable, sociable, friendly and understanding enough to rise above differences of opinion and exalt God in each other. People don't agree on subjects of education, pollution, international affairs, etc.; but that is no reason why they can't live together in harmony, peace and understanding.

I pointed out to her that while her attorney opposed and seemingly denounced the fallacious reasoning of the opposing counsel, and while arguing and disputing on points of law, apparently they were emotionally and spiritually mature enough to respect each other's opinions and to rise above the disputations in the court room and subsequently join in fellowship, laughter and goodwill with each other at lunch. This demonstrated that they were emotionally and spiritually mature. I said to her, "Your attorney is not selling you down the river; neither is he agreeing with the arguments of the opposing counsel.

"Come to terms in your own mind. Meet the problems head on; know that the law of Infinite justice and harmony is operating for you and all concerned and that Divine love is guiding your attorney, revealing to him what he needs to know. Claim that Divine love brings about a perfect Divine adjustment and Divine solution."

She perceived the truth about what was said and emphatically claimed that the principle of justice was operating on her behalf and the behalf of all concerned and that Divine order prevails. In a few weeks' time, her attorney won the case and she was freed. False allegations and affidavits had been filed against her, but the truth prevailed.

A Visit to Washington, D.C.

Some years ago I was invited by Dr. Grace Faus to speak at the Divine Science Church at Washington, D.C. After a series of lectures, I was invited by a prominent attorney to one of the exclusive clubs, where he introduced me to two Senators, saying: "These men are deadly enemies on the floor of the Senate, but here they relax, play cards, have cocktails and enjoy themselves."

The four of us had an animated conversation about the country, politics, crime, etc. Frankly, I disagreed with nearly everything they said about poverty, share-the-wealth programs, crime and war; and I told them so. However, I could see their point of view, based upon their background, early training, political indoctrination and theological beliefs. Nevertheless, we had a delightful two hours together.

You don't agree with anything irrational, unreasonable and unscientific that insults your intelligence.

Any political belief, such as share-the-wealth or any teaching which contravenes the Golden Rule and the law of love, must of necessity be false. My host, the attorney, said that more money should be appropriated to banish the slums, with which I entirely disagreed, explaining to him a simple mental and spiritual law: All the money in America could not banish the slums until we banish the slums in the mind of man. Cleanliness is next to Godliness. Furthermore, I added: You can take thousands from the slums and put them in up-to-date, modern apartments with all the appurtenances added, and in a few months these apartments will be worse than the slums they left. As within (the mind), so without (the objective world).

I said to one of the Senators: "Senator, you could arrange at gun point to take all the money from the wealthy people in Washington and share it equally with all the so-called poor people in Washington and all those in the skid row section of the city; but if you knew the law of mind, you would realize that the money taken from the rich would in a few weeks find its way back into the pockets from which it was taken. The reason is that wealth is a state of mind. You can't possess anything except by right of consciousness. The rich have the mental equivalent established in their subconscious; therefore, they demonstrate wealth. The poor can't retain the money given them because they don't possess it mentally. In other words, they have the mental equivalent of poverty, lack and limitation. This is why the old aphorism is true: The rich get richer and the poor get poorer.

All three disagreed with me, but we parted the best of friends, and I have a standing invitation to visit all three any time I am in Washington, D.C. However, I don't have to agree with their foolish, idiotic beliefs.

The Meaning of the Uttermost Farthing

Verse 26, quoted at the beginning of this chapter, sounds ominous, and one girl in our recent class on the Inner Meaning of the Healings of the Bible said to me: "Doesn't that mean we must go to Purgatory where we suffer for a time before we go to Heaven?" I explained to her that she is already in Heaven, which is the Infinite Spirit in which we live, move and have our being; and God, or Spirit, lives, moves and has His Being in us.

Also, when your mind is at peace and you are in tune with the Infinite, you are, relatively speaking, in Heaven, which also means harmony, peace, poise and tranquility. Purgatory is a state of suffering which takes place in our mind because of our misuse of the laws of mind. We suffer from our hates, jealousies, envies and negative thinking until we get a new insight and a new understanding of the laws of mind and the way of the Infinite within us. We remain in purgatory or misery until we purge or cleanse our mind by forgiving ourselves and others and filling our mind with the truths of God; then a healing follows. This is the way out of so-called purgatory, or pain and misery.

How She Paid the Last Farthing

A widow with whom I conversed in Salt Lake City, Utah, told me that she suffered from a worrisome growth. The doctor, after examination, told her to come back in a week and he would take a biopsy. She said, "I know that this growth could be resentment or hatred, but as far as I know, I don't resent anybody and I don't hate myself. I pray regularly and practice the science of the mind." She agreed though that the resentment or suppressed rage could be of an unconscious nature and that she knew there must be a poison pocket somewhere in her subconscious mind.

I suggested that as an experiment she ask her subconscious this question prior to sleep: "Infinite Intelligence reveals to me whom I should forgive, whether myself or someone else." Really, all forgiveness in the final analysis is self-forgiveness, because when we have forgiven ourselves and we are at peace within, we will automatically be at peace and have goodwill to all.

The following night after the lecture in Salt Lake City, she came to me and said: "I had a very vivid dream last night. In the dream I saw my sister, and I was shouting at her, saying, 'I no longer hate you.' Then I woke up screaming out loud. I had received my answer." Some years previously this woman had been engaged to a young engineer. Apparently, her sister enticed him away and they got married. At that time it was quite a traumatic shock to her, and she hated her sister as a result. They were not on speaking terms for several years until a few days prior to her demise. At that time she had prayed for forgiveness and thought she had released her sister.

After awakening, she sat down quietly and affirmed: "I forgive myself for harboring this suppressed anger and hatred. I fully and freely forgive you now. I loose you and let you go. I know in my heart that your journey is from glory to glory, from wisdom to wisdom, from strength to strength and from light to a greater light. It is done. It is finished, and established in God. I am free and you are free."

She said that in her dream she knew it was a catharsis, a cleansing and a release of a psychic poison pocket which she had repressed and refused to meet and overcome. In other words, she had brushed it under the rug. Due to the fact that it was a negative, destructive emotion, it had to have an outlet and, therefore, appeared as a growth.

After her prayer of forgiveness, and while dressing for the class in the evening, she noticed that the growth had broken and was oozing. She called her physician, who said to come in at once, which she did. He told her that it was dissolving, that there was no malignancy, and that it would completely disappear. She could not get a healing while the poison pocket was in her subconscious. She had to pay the full price, which was complete forgiveness of herself and her sister. That is the meaning of paying the uttermost farthing.

The Prophets of Doom and Gloom

Love never faileth: but whether there be prophecies, they shall fail; whether there be tongues, they shall cease; whether there be knowledge, it shall vanish away (I Corinthians 13:8).

The prophets of doom and gloom are rampant everywhere, particularly on the West Coast. Some predict earthquakes and that the State of California will sink into the sea. When people ask me about it, I ask them: "Can you swim? If so, there will be no problem. You can swim to the next state."

Others predict Armageddon, a nuclear holocaust. Many others predict the end of the world, the second coming, world famine, overpopulation, etc. Look how often all these prognosticators have had to eat crow. All the economic forecasters have been proven wrong. California is still one of the states and seems to be quite substantial.

The second coming has not taken place, nor will it ever take place. It can't. The meaning of the second coming is the coming of love, peace, wisdom, understanding and goodwill in the minds and hearts of men. It is the birth of God and His love in our hearts and in our actions. The Divine Presence can't come or go. It is Omnipresent, and being Omnipresent, It must be within you.

How could It come or go? That's pure balderdash and rank stupidity. There is no man coming out of the clouds in a chariot with angels to save you or anybody else. The savior is within you—the Presence of God.

You know very well that if the fortune tellers could predict accurately the stocks that would go up in value, they would be rolling in wealth. Actually, they could make fabulous fortunes. Learn to predict your own future. The law of life is the law of belief . . . *Whatsoever ye shall ask in prayer, believing, ye shall receive* (Matthew 21:22).

Believe that God is guiding you. Believe in the goodness and love of God. Believe in Divine right action. Believe in Divine law and order governing your life. Believe that God is prospering you beyond your fondest dreams. Believe this truth: *Thou art my hiding place; thou shalt preserve me from trouble; thou shalt compass me about with songs of deliverance . . .* (Psalm 32:7).

Dwelling on these truths, you live above the mass mind. Your future is your present habitual thinking and imagery made manifest on the screen of space. You mold and fashion your own destiny. Nothing is predestined or foreordained. Your faith in God is your fortune and your future.

His Opinion Was All Wrong

A junior executive complained to me that the vice president of his firm was blocking his promotion and that that was the reason he was passed over twice for promotion. I explained to him, however, that he must understand that every man promotes himself, the reason being that if any man contemplates promotion, expansion, achievement and advancement, he is in accordance with the principles of life, which is forever seeking expression at higher levels through him. The Bible says: . . . *I have set before thee an open door, and no man can shut it . . .* (Revelation 3:8).

Marcus Aurelius said: "Let your opinion be still." This young executive learned that he was transferring the Power within himself to another man, thereby making the latter some sort of a god and, in effect, decreeing that the vice president of his organization was greater than the Infinite Presence within him. He saw the absurdity of his attitude and the foolishness of his own opinion.

He decreed knowingly, feelingly and with understanding: "Pro- motion is mine, advancement is mine, expansion along all lines is mine. Infinite Intelligence guides me, directs me and opens up a new door of expression for me where I am expressing myself at my highest level, and I receive a marvelous compensation."

He reiterated these truths for about four or five minutes several times a day, making sure that he did not subsequently deny what he affirmed. He also pictured the president of the company congratulating him on his outstanding achievement and success on behalf of the organization. His mental picture agreed with his affirmation, and at the end of a month he was promoted to executive assistant to the president of the organization.

This young man realized that his changed mental attitude changed everything.

The Real Adversaries

The adversary is not really something outside yourself. The adversaries are fear, superstition, ignorance, resentment, jealousy, hate, self-condemnation and hostility. These negative thoughts are your real enemies, and they generate destructive, negative emotions which lodge in the recesses of your deeper mind, creating all manner of disease, lack and limitation.

Meet them boldly in your mind and eradicate them. Ask yourself: Where did these thoughts come from? Do they belong in my mind? Is there a principle behind them? What are they doing to me? Are they not created by myself? You know the answer to all of these questions.

All you have to do is to quiet your mind and affirm boldly: "I forgive myself for generating these thoughts." Then fill your mind with these truths: "Divine love fills my soul. Divine peace flows through me. Divine love heals me. I radiate love and goodwill to all those around me and to all people everywhere." Affirm these truths out loud for about fifteen minutes and you will expunge from your mind all the negativity. When any negative thought comes to your mind, eliminate it immediately by affirming, "God's love fills my soul."

It is not what is said or done to you that matters; it is your reaction to it. It is your own thought about it. You can bless the person and say, "I loose you. I let you go, and God be with you." It is your own thought that makes you depressed or causes you to suffer from what is said or done. Cease judging situations and people and you will cease being troubled, excited, agitated and perturbed.

Be Your Age

A woman forty years of age complained that her mother had always told her she was stupid, awkward and retarded and that she was here to suffer. The mother had passed on to the next dimension, however, and she was still resenting her and blaming her because she hadn't married or made her mark in the world.

It was true that she was conditioned or programmed negatively by her mother, but she had been taking classes on metaphysics and had acquired an excellent knowledge of the powers of her subconscious. I pointed out to her that she had no one to blame but herself; that she had a lot of head knowledge, but that it must become heart knowledge. In other words, the truths of life must be incorporated in her subconscious mind.

Accordingly, she began to fill her subconscious mind with life- giving patterns regularly and systematically and consequently succeeded in transforming her whole life. There is no time or space in the mind-principle, and the minute she began to busy her conscious mind with the eternal verities, there was an automatic response from her subconscious mind.

The first thing she had to do was to release her mother, to loose her and let her go, knowing that what you resent you bind and what you love you release. She decreed: "I forgive myself completely. I fully and freely forgive my mother, and I radiate love and peace to her. I know and rejoice that the Light of God shines in her and that her journey is onward, upward and God ward. I loose her and let her go." Whenever the thought of her mother came to her mind, she would silently bless her by affirming. "God loves you, Mother."

Forgiveness is for your own sake more than the other. One of our prominent psychiatrists in Los Angeles recently said: "I make my patients realize they are responsible for their actions, spiritual awakening and maturity." Cease blaming father, mother, sister, brother, the government, the weather or the fan. Admit that you allowed the negative thoughts of others to influence you or disturb you. You are the only thinker in your world, and others are not responsible for the way you think about them. You are.

An Interesting Experience

I once invited a sister of mine to visit Ireland with me. She is a nun in St. Mary's Convent in England, where she teaches Latin, French and mathematics. We were driven to various interesting places by a cousin of ours. We visited the old homestead, which is now in ruins; but the old school house still stands, though not in "use. We walked through the area covered with weeds, trees, plants and wild growth of all kinds. A few days later our cousin told us that we were walking through poison ivy, and we had brushed it aside with our hands several times. We didn't know it was poison ivy, though, and, obviously, it had no effect upon us. All three of us had a good laugh about it.

And God said . . . let them have dominion over the fish of the sea, and over the fowl of the air, and over the cattle, and over all the earth, and over every creeping thing that creepeth upon the earth (Genesis 1:26).

Man has been given dominion over the beasts of the field. That is why man can tame the wild horse or the lion or tiger. His conscious mind controls the subjective mind of the animals. Man has control of every creeping thing also, such as bacteria, germs, animals, birds, plants, etc.

Man must exercise his dominion and cease giving power to the ragweed, pollen, Timothy grass, etc. In other words, give power to the Creator within you; not to the created thing. God pronounced everything he had made as good and very good. Good and evil are the movements of our own mind relative to everything God hath created and made. There is nothing good or bad, but thinking makes it so. The Primal Cause is within man, and we must cease conferring power or transferring qualities to outer things which they do not possess.

You Can Program Constructively

A school teacher who is a student in our Bible classes, where we teach the inner meaning of the Bible, and not from the historical standpoint, told me that when she tells a student that she believes in him, expects great things from him, that he is brilliant and has a tremendous future, and she has faith in him, he responds accordingly. She believes her students will learn rapidly, and according to her belief is it done unto her. Her faith in the power within them is communicated telepathically to them.

How a College Student Responded

Robby Wright, who handles my radio program on Saturday morning every week, told me last week that his part-time work as a consultant in electronics nets him $350 weekly. This is exceptionally good for a young man of twenty-one years of age who is in his third year in college.

A few years ago I told him: "Robby, you have a fabulous mind, full of creative ideas. You are a wizard in mathematics and electronics, and you will reach fabulous heights and bring forth new and outstanding discoveries." He accepted all that and uses his subconscious mind every night by filling it with constructive thoughts and directing it to reveal to him new and original ideas which will bless humanity. He has perfected two new devices along electronic lines that are revolutionary and will ultimately make fortunes for the company he is working for.

The Handgun Is In the Mind of Man

If you are a mother, father or teacher, you can program the subconscious mind of your son or daughter constructively. It is the quiet mind that gets things done. People who are running around saying we must fight cancer, tuberculosis, poverty, crime and hand guns are magnifying the problems in their own minds and impressing their subconscious with the negativity.

Instead of getting all exercised and seething about hand guns, write to your congressman and tell him to pass a mandatory sentence of twenty-five years for those who murder, and you won't need to worry about hand guns. Murder is in the mind of man; not in a piece of machinery. He is responsible and must take the consequences. It is wrong to release a murderer or felon who, when he is paroled, murders and rapes again.

Come to a decision in your mind based on common sense. Understand why people do what they do and establish peace in your own mind. You become what you contemplate, and if you are a woman going around calling men "chauvinistic pigs," then you are revealing your hatred of yourself and projecting that self-loathing onto others.

You become what you contemplate, and it is the nature of

love, as it is the nature of hate, to change you into the image and likeness of that which you contemplate.

Learn to agree with thine adversary. Remember: *And God shall wipe away all tears from their eyes . . .* (Revelations 21:4). Come to a clear understanding in your mind and realize that there is no one to change but yourself. Stop trying to change the world. Nothing is forever. Grief, sorrow, sickness, etc., all pass away. Joy displaces sadness, tears give way to gladness. After the storm comes the calm. When depressed or sad, focus your attention on the solution, the way out, the happy ending, and all the power of the God-head will flow to the focal point of your attention, and you will thus experience the joy of the answered prayer.

10

How to Pray Effectively

And it was told Tamar, saying, Behold thy father in law goeth up to Timnath to shear his sheep.

And she put her widow's garments off from her, and covered her with a veil, and wrapped herself, and sat in an open place, which is by the way to Timnath; for she saw that Shelah was grown, and she was not given unto him to wife.

When Judah saw her, he thought her to be an harlot; because she had covered her face.

And he turned unto her by the way, and said, Go to, I pray thee, let me come in unto thee; (for he knew not that she was his daughter in law.) And she said, What wilt thou give me, that thou mayest come in unto me?

And he said, I will send thee a kid from the flock. And she said, Wilt thou give me a pledge, till thou send it?

And he said, What pledge shall I give thee? And she said, Thy signet, and thy bracelets, and thy staff that is in thine hand. And he gave it her, and came in unto her, and she conceived by him.

And she arose, and went away, and laid by her veil from her, and put on the garments of her widowhood.

And Judah sent the kid by the hand of his friend the Adullamite, to receive his pledge from the woman's hand: but he found her not.

Then he asked the men of that place, saying, where is the harlot, that was openly by the way side? And they said, there was no harlot in this place.

And he returned to Judah, and said, I cannot find her; and also the men of the place said, that there was no harlot in this place.

And Judah said, let her take it to her, lest we be shamed; behold, I sent this kid, and thou hast not found her.

And it came to pass about three months after, that it was told Judah, saying, Tamar thy daughter in law hath played the harlot; and also, behold, she is with child by whoredom. And Judah said, Bring her forth, and let her be burnt.

When she was brought forth, she sent to her father in law, saying, By the man, whose these are, am I with child: and she said, Discern, I pray thee, whose are these, the signet, and bracelets, and staff (Genesis 38:13-25).

Judah means to praise Jehovah. Whatever you praise, you increase through the law of mind. Tamar means victory, conquest, moral righteousness, excellence and goodness. Tamar also means a palm tree, which, symbolically speaking, represents the cherished desire of your heart. A man bent on achieving the desired objective, his fairest possession, gave a pledge in the form of three securities or symbols—a signet ring, bracelets and a staff.

A ring is a circle and is a symbol of Infinity, or God, which has no beginning or end. It is also a symbol of love and of the unbroken married life. It symbolizes your Divine marriage, your mental and spiritual union with the Infinite. It means that you give all your allegiance, devotion and loyalty to the One Power within you, while knowing It to be Supreme and Omnipotent.

The symbol of the ring is to emphasize the importance of changing the focus of man's belief from matter and external conditions to Spirit, the Cause of all. Isaiah stresses the great truth that there is only One Power of creation, and it is I AM, or consciousness, awareness, mind or imagery. There is no other creative power. Your mind must reach an absolute conviction regarding the One Power, which is beyond all argument, disputation and comparison; then you reach a point of real faith and confidence, which is your rest in God.

I am Alpha and Omega, the beginning and the ending, saith the Lord . . . (Revelation 1:8). Your desire to be, to do, and to have is the beginning, and fulfillment is the end. The beginning and end take place in your own mind. From now on, when you think of a ring, it will remind you of steadfastness and fidelity. Bracelets are symbolic of being bound to God in faith and confidence. They also symbolize adornment or dressing for God.

When you are clothed with the garment of truth and confidence that the word which you speak shall come to pass, you are wearing the proper bracelets. *Thou shall also decree a thing, and it shall be established unto thee: and the light shall shine upon thy ways* (Job 22:28). Your word, Biblically speaking, is your thought and feeling fused together; in other words, it is your conviction that what you decreed will be made manifest.

This deals with the law of correspondence, or the law of reciprocal relationship, which means that whatever you impress in your subconscious, the latter reproduces accordingly. In other words, your impression becomes an expression. The bracelets represent, therefore, to you that you are bound to the law.

But his delight is in the law of the Lord; and in his law doth he meditate day and night. And he shall be like a tree planted by the rivers of water, that bringeth forth his fruit in his season; his leaf also shall not wither; and whatsoever he doeth shall prosper (Psalms 1:2-3).

The law is that you are what you contemplate; whatever you feel is true about yourself is expressed as form, function, experience and event. The law of life is the law of belief. You are belief expressed. To believe is to accept something as true. Believe in the goodness and the abundance of God in the land of the living.

The staff mentioned in the Biblical story represents unbending discipline, on which it is an advantage to lean. The Psalmist says in the 23rd Psalm: *Thy rod and thy staff they comfort me* (Psalm 23:4). The Psalmist is cognizant of the fact that sheep are helpless, dumb animals and possess no weapon to ward off attackers or wild beasts of the field.

The staff in ancient times was about six or seven feet long. The end was formed into the shape of a crook, and in case one of the sheep slipped or fell into a ravine, the shepherd could reach down with his staff and lift the sheep up. All this means is that we lean on God, knowing that when we call He will answer. As the Psalmist says, He is . . . *A very present help in trouble* (Psalm 46:1).

The writer of Genesis says that when you pray you are being put to the test. Can someone or some circumstance dissuade you from your allegiance and loyalty to the One Power (the ring), your faith and conviction that It is the Only Presence, Power, Cause and Substance (bracelets), and your understanding of Its responsiveness to you when you call upon It?

If someone ridicules what you believe in, e.g., you may have a so-called incurable condition and you are praying about it, knowing that the Infinite Healing Presence which made you can heal you and is healing you now, when others mock you and tell you how foolish you are, do you remain steadfast in your faith, or do you permit them to cause you to waiver in your faith or conviction?

Supposing you have an ideal or outstanding goal for yourself or the country at large, the fulfillment of which would bless humanity, and let us assume that some people offered to bribe you with honors, money, fame, attractive power and position. If this bait were proffered you, would you yield or adhere to your ideal? If you yield to the blandishment and temptation of the world, the pledge you gave in your prayer life is not safe. In this story, it says Judah sent a kid with which to recover the pledge from the woman, just to see if she were really faithful. You prove yourself unworthy when you exchange things that really matter for things that do not, preferring counterfeits to genuine goods.

Genuine goods are fidelity to the One Power, love, goodwill, honesty, integrity, harmony and confidence in all things good. We must realize that our acts correspond with our words, for a word is a thought expressed, and our actions are preceded by our thoughts. We must exercise a strict discipline of right thought, right feeling and right action. *I sent the kid and thou hast not found her* (Genesis 38:23). The person whose faith is sealed in God, knowing that all honors and all growth come from within, cannot be bribed or induced to turn away from the One, the Beautiful and the Good.

You can put this drama to pass in your life. Tamar is his daughter in law, which means that with which you would like to be mentally and emotionally united. You are married to your estimate of yourself. It is called a daughter because it represents your feeling nature. How do you feel about yourself? Do you want to feel happy? Do you want to feel successful? Do you want to feel sad or depressed? Do you want to feel wealthy? If you feel wealth, you will become wealthy. The feeling of wealth produces wealth. If you feel yourself to be successful, you will be. You can participate in any state you wish simply by feeling the reality of that state.

Tamar is the palm tree. As you know, the sight of a palm tree in the desert indicates refreshment and an oasis. Your goal in life is the palm tree; therefore, the story is really about yourself. You want to become grander and greater than you are at present.

You are told in the Bible story that she dresses in the veils of a harlot. The latter is a symbolic expression representing your subconscious, which will give to you whatever you impress upon it, good or bad, in the same way as a harlot, literally speaking, serves all men and asks no questions.

In the story, her father in law, King Judah, offers her a kid to be intimate with her, *and she said, What wilt thou give me, that thou mayest come in unto me?* (Genesis 38:16). *And he said, What pledge shall I give thee? And she said, Thy signet, and thy bracelets, and thy staff that is in thine hand. And he gave it her, and came in unto her, and she conceived by him* (Genesis 38:18).

You have but one gift to give. God is the giver and the gift, and God indwells you. Therefore, that being true, all you can give is your faith in God; and according to your faith is it done unto you. Actually, you give everything to yourself, for the source of all things is within you.

You give yourself wisdom by affirming: "The wisdom of God anoints my intellect, and I am illumined from On High." You give yourself wealth by claiming: "God's wealth is circulating in my life, and there is always a Divine surplus." You give yourself peace by tuning in with the Infinite, which lies stretched in smiling repose, and affirming feelingly and knowingly: "God's river of peace fills my mind, my heart, and my whole being." You give yourself strength by claiming boldly: "The power of the Almighty flows through me, vitalizing, healing and energizing my whole being."

You remember the creative act stated in Genesis, which portrayed Adam begetting the woman (feeling nature) out of himself. You can fashion and picture in your mind the object of your desire and feel the reality of it. As you sustain that feeling, it will gel within you, and your subconscious will bring it to pass.

Judah is yourself, when you exalt the power of God within you. You have but one gift to give, as the ring, the bracelets and the staff symbolize, for these represent the symbols of your kingship. You can't give the Infinite anything but recognition and loyalty. Man oftentimes tries to bargain with the Infinite by promising to give up drinking, for example, if his boy is healed or to build a church if his prayer is answered. But there is only one thing you can give God, and that is your faith and conviction, knowing that Infinite Intelligence responds to your conviction and never fails. The ring, the bracelet and the staff are symbols of kingship. When you give these three you are giving yourself; namely, recognition, faith and acceptance.

Become King Judah and realize and know that before you can know and feel the reality of your Tamar (desire), you must impregnate your subconscious by claiming and feeling the reality of your desire. As you continue to give your attention and loyalty to your ideal, it will gestate in the darkness of your subconscious, and you will have given of yourself, because you poured life, meaning and love into your ideal. When you become filled to capacity with the feeling of being what you long to be, your subconscious will dramatize and objectify your ideal on the screen of space.

If you want security in life, it is foolish to bask in the limelight of those who are wealthy and feel secure. You become secure by feeling and knowing that God is the Overshadowing Presence

Which watches over you, guides and protects you and supplies all your needs according to His riches in glory. Likewise, if you want to be healthy, vital, strong and powerful, you must realize that climate, diet and vitamins are not enough. You must realize that God, the Ever Living One, the All Wise One, is within you, vitalizing, healing, restoring and vivifying your whole being; and you will then get a response from the Infinite, Which is the Source of all life. Don't look outside or to created things for health; always go to the Source of Life itself.

You want to grow, expand and be lifted up in this world. There is no use in associating with royalty, presidents, titled and affluent people. That association won't make you feel noble, dignified or outstanding in your field of endeavor. The way to become noble and dignified is to realize that you are a son or daughter of the Infinite, and to affirm and feel: "I am illumined and inspired. I am lifted up spiritually, and I am expressing more and more of God's love, light, truth and beauty. I am conscious of being an offspring of God, and I am moving onward, upward and Godward." Keep on knowing these truths, and walk the earth feeling the truth of what you affirm, and you will become noble, dignified and more Godlike every day.

An actress friend of mine in England imagined herself as being absolutely outstanding, and she constantly pictured in her mind's eye her husband saying to her, "You are wonderful. Your movies in Spain, France, etc. are fabulously successful." As she gave allegiance, devotion and attention to that mental image, she became absolutely out- standing, and in the years that followed, she has written me many wonderful letters about her tremendous success.

When you begin to claim and feel that you now are what you long to be, you are Tamar in the Bible. All the stories of the Bible take place within the mind of the individual man. All the characters of the Bible, like the characters in Shakespeare's plays, live in you.

Know that your consciousness is the only Reality. Then know what you desire to be. Then imagine and feel that you now are what you long to be and remain faithful to your mental picture, living the role, and it will come to pass, and the Light of God will shine upon your ways.

There Is Only One

Take note of the categorical and absolute announcement in Isaiah: . . . *I am God and there is none else* (Isaiah 45:22) . . . *Thou hast said in thine heart, I am, and none else beside me* (Isaiah 47:10). *I am the Lord: that is my name: and my glory will I not give to another, neither my praise to graven images* (Isaiah 42:8) . . . *I am God, and there is none like me* (Isaiah 46:9).

Recently I told a young woman of seventy-five who desired to get married to image herself in my study and hear me saying the words, "I now pronounce you man and wife." These words indicated to her that the ceremony was over and that she was already married in her mind. She made sure that she attributed as much reality to that mental image as she did to the tree outside her door. Then I pointed out that the image she dramatized in her mind would come to pass joyously and triumphantly.

She dramatized this mental movie every night, giving as much reality to her mental image as she did to the big tree outside her home. In a week's time her neighbor, a widower, proposed to her, and the author had the pleasure of performing the ceremony . . . *And calleth those things which be not as though they were* (Romans 4:17).

This woman said to me that for the first time in her life she realized that the beginning and the end are the same. It is true: End and beginning are always one. If you contemplate and visualize the end, you have willed the means to the realization of the end. Cause and effect are one.

She proved to herself that the dramatization of her mental image was just as real as the marriage ceremony in which she later participated. If you enter into a new enterprise or assignment with the feeling of faith, confidence and victory, that attitude predicts the end, which will be successful and triumphant. The idea precedes the manifestation. Begin with joy in your heart and the end will be joyous.

Once you realize that God is Consciousness, Awareness, the Spirit within you, you realize that there are no real enemies in the external world, no antagonists, and nothing to oppose or fight with It. The minute you begin to claim in your mind that which you want to be, to do, or to have, there is a response from an Almighty Power, which moves on your behalf; then nothing can prevent you from attaining the cherished desire of your heart. Claim what you want to be with a feeling of joy and satisfaction, and your deeper mind will bring it to pass in Divine order.

11

How the Bible Looks at Jealousy and Envy

For jealousy is the rage of a man: therefore he will not spare in the day of vengeance (Proverbs 6:34).

Set me as a seal upon thine heart, as a seal upon thine arm: for love is strong as death; jealousy is cruel as the grave: the coals thereof are coals of fire, which hath a most vehement flame (Song of Solomon 8:6).

"Trifles light as air, are to the jealous confirmation strong as proof of holy writ" (Shakespeare).

"Jealousy sees things always with magnifying glasses which make little things large, of dwarfs giants, of suspicions truths" (Cervantes).

"Jealousy is the injured lover's hell" (Milton).

"The jealous man poisons his own banquet and then eats it.

"Oh, beware of jealousy; it is the green-eyed monster, which doth mock the meat it feeds on" (Shakespeare).

"Jealousy," says Rochefoucauld, "is in some sort rational and just; it aims at the preservation of a good which we think belongs to us." It is in this sense that God is said to be a jealous God, because he is earnestly and, as it were, passionately desirous of our supreme love, reverence and service.

In our modern, everyday language, we speak of a jealous person as one who feels resentment against another because of his success, worldly achievements or monetary advantages. A jealous person is inclined to be troubled by suspicions or fears of rivalry, unfaithfulness, etc., as in love or aims.

The Bible, in Exodus 20:5, says: . . . *For I the Lord thy God am a jealous God* . . . This means that you must recognize the Living Spirit Almighty as supreme and omnipotent and refuse to give power to any created thing. In other words, you should not worship a created thing; you must give all allegiance, loyalty and devotion to the One Presence and Power within you, called I AM, or Spirit.

For example, if you are looking for promotion or advancement and you say to yourself: "The boss is blocking my good; but for him I would be promoted and receive greater emoluments," at that moment you have exalted him, a false god. Actually, you are making the boss a god and denying the One Source from Whom all blessings flow. Your subconscious mind knows that your loyalty is divided and consequently does not respond.

You are like the double-minded man, unstable in all your ways. On the one hand he is affirming that God is the Source of his supply, meeting all his needs, and then in the next breath he is resenting his employer for not promoting him and increasing his salary. You must never give power to any person, place or thing, for actually you are transferring the power within you to externals. You must give exclusive devotion and loyalty to the One Power within you, Which responds according to the nature of your thoughts and belief.

He Thought Vitamins Would Heal Him

A man who had ulcers refused to take any medication from his doctor. His faith was in Vitamin C; but he had ulcerated thoughts of jealousy and resentment toward a partner. He was also envious and resentful of his wife, who was making more money than he was.

I explained to him that his faith and confidence should be in the One Supreme Power—the Source of all life. Food is important, vitamins are important, but not preeminently so. You don't put food, diet or vitamins before the Infinite Healing Presence—the only Healing Power there is.

His healing prayer was: "I forgive myself for harboring negative, jealous thoughts, and I radiate love, peace and goodwill to my wife and partner. God's healing love saturates my whole being. God's river of peace saturates my mind and heart. Whenever a jealous or envious thought comes to me, I will affirm: 'God's love fills my soul.'"

He practiced this discipline, and in a few weeks' time his ulcers disappeared. He realized that ulcerated thoughts of jealousy, envy, ill will and fear caused his ulcers. By reversing the process, and by contemplating harmony, love, wholeness, goodwill and peace, a healing took place. He had to give recognition to the Creator alone, and not to His manifestations. Always look to the Primary Cause, the Source of life itself, not the secondary cause. A doctor can prescribe a good diet for you, but then realize that whatever you eat or drink is transmuted into beauty, order, symmetry and proportion.

He Said the Planets Blocked Him

A fledgling writer had his manuscript rejected by six organizations, and he said to me that a reader told him the reason was due to a malefic configuration of Saturn and other planets in his chart. I said to him that he would be far better off if he had never heard of Saturn.

God is immutable law, and whatever we impress on our subconscious mind is expressed on the screen of space. He began to understand that he had been the victim of a hypnotic suggestion which he accepted. He was giving power to a planet instead of to the God Who made it as well as the whole universe. There is only One Being, One Power; and a spiritual minded thinker does not give power to the phenomenalistic world. He gives all allegiance and worship to the One Power. *I am the Lord: that is my name: and my glory will I not give to another, neither my praise to graven images* (Isaiah 42:8).

I read his manuscript. It was very good, and his writing was worthy of acceptance and approval. I suggested that he get in touch with the president of a book publishing company, a friend of the author, and I added: "I'm sure he will see the value of it."

I suggested that he pray as follows: "Infinite Intelligence opens up the perfect way for the acceptance, manufacture and sale of my manuscript; and this man I am going to see is God's man. The Spirit in me speaks to the Spirit in him, and there are harmony, peace and understanding between us. I release the manuscript to him, and it is God in action, which is all around harmony and peace."

The president of the publishing company accepted his manuscript. This man predicated his success upon remembrance of the One Power and not on the created thing. He realized he was not a victim of a malefic configuration of planets in the sky, but that he was a victim of a negative suggestion. The planets have no power, but if you believe they have power over you, it is done unto you as you believe. The law of life is the law of belief . . . *As thou hast believed, so be it done unto thee* . . . (Matthew 8:13).

There is a mass mind or race mind belief that a person born under a certain sign will have certain characteristics, proclivities and talents. It isn't because a man is born under the sign of Taurus that he has certain traits and tendencies; but, rather, it is the mass mind belief about that date or season of the year.

God indwells every person, and any person can contact the Divine Presence within and transform his life. You mold and fashion your own destiny, and it is written: . . . *Whatsoever a man soweth, that shall he also reap* (Galatians 6:7). *For as he thinketh in his heart, so is he* . . . (Proverbs 23:7).

Your thought and feeling represent the Father within, Which doeth the works. Your heart in the Bible represents your subconscious mind; and whatever you impregnate in your subconscious comes forth as expression, condition and events. Phineas Parkhurst Quimby in 1847 said, "Man is belief expressed."

What do you believe? Your habitual thinking, or your regular train of thoughts will cause you to arrive, like a train, at a certain destination.

Programming Your Subconscious Mind

Today we read a lot about programming of computers. The computer responds according to whatever is fed into it. When you were young, there is the possibility that you were told a great number of things which were false. Perhaps one of your parents said to you: "Your brother is much smarter than you. Why don't you be like him? He is an angel." This probably gave rise to jealousy and competition as well as resentment.

You were born with only two fears: fear of falling and fear of noise. These represent nature's protective mechanism. Quimby said that every child is like a white tablet upon which everyone who comes along scribbles something. Modern day educators term this a tabula rasa, or blank tablet. Remember, you were born with the Infinite Spirit, or God, within you—the very life of you.

Always ask yourself this simple question: "What did I inherit from God?" If your subconscious has been programmed negatively, you can reverse it by filling your subconscious with life-giving patterns, such as: "God's love fills my soul. God's peace saturates my whole being. The harmony, light, and glory of the Infinite saturate my whole being, and I am illumined from On High."

Do this regularly at least three or four times a day. When a negative thought comes to you, chop off its head by affirming: "Divine love fills my soul." Prayer is a habit, but it is a very good habit. Suppose you have been trained in the wrong way to play the piano or drive a car. You can, by practice, unlearn the old way and play or drive the right way. Many dogs in the First and Second World Wars were trained to kill, but after the war they were retrained to become lovers of mankind again.

Two Wonderful Mantras

Many men and women, at my suggestion, use this mantra every morning for about 15 minutes and also at night for about 15 minutes. They close their eyes, relax on a couch, and talk to their bodies as follows: "My toes are relaxed, my feet are relaxed, my ankles are relaxed, the calves of my legs are relaxed, my knees and thighs are relaxed, my abdominal muscles are relaxed, my heart and lungs are relaxed, my spine is relaxed, my hands and arms are relaxed, my neck is relaxed, my brain is relaxed, my face is relaxed, my whole being is completely relaxed, and I am at peace."

After relaxing their bodies in the above manner, they silently whisper to themselves for about 15 minutes: "God's love fills my soul." They repeat this over and over again like a lullaby in the morning and for about 15 minutes prior to sleep. They have told me that it is a wonderful way to recharge their mental and spiritual batteries. They accomplish more. Many have told me that their blood pressure became normal, they experienced far less tension during the day, their health improved, jealousy and envy disappeared, and they became more affable, amiable, cordial and genial. The simple mantra, "God's love fills my soul," has worked wonders in their lives.

He that loveth not knoweth not God; for God is love (I John 4:8). The practice of this mantra dissolves all jealousy and envy.

Another Wonderful Mantra

Many use this wonderful, healing and vitalizing mantra: "God's peace fills my soul." They use it the same way as the preceding one, 15 minutes morning and evening prior to sleep. They sleep in peace and wake in joy. Moreover, they find peace in their home, office, and in their relations with others. They also find peace in their pocket books, because when you tune in with the God of peace within you, all things are added to you.

Thou wilt keep him in perfect peace, whose mind is stayed on thee: because he trusteth in thee (Isaiah 26:3). *Peace I leave with you, my peace I give unto you: not as the world giveth, give I unto you . . .* (John 14:27). *For God is not the author of confusion, but of peace, as in all churches of the saints* (I Corinthians 14:33). *Let the peace of God rule in your hearts . . .* (Colossians 3:15).

The practice of the above mantra, "God's peace fills my soul," brings peace into your home, your heart, your business and all phases of your life. The ancients said that peace is the power at the heart of God. When you are presented with any difficulty, challenge or problem, during the day, silently affirm, "God's peace fills my soul." You will be amazed how quickly the solution or the creative idea will present itself, which reveals the answer. New, original, creative ideas will come to you during each day, and you will find yourself vivified, recharged, and God intoxicated.

The above-mentioned mantra is the Divine antibody. The habitual use of this mantra does away with all resentment, hostility, anger, etc. Equanimity, serenity and tranquility become a living part of you, as the apple becomes a part of your blood stream.

He Said, "I Am Not Jealous"

Your emotions govern you. Emotion follows thought. You can't visualize an emotion, but you can look back at an old scene, an old law suit or some old hurt and grievance and imagine the particular scene again. Of course, you will generate a destructive emotion and reinfect yourself all over again. When the old hurt comes to your mind, practice the law of substitution and affirm: "God's peace fills my soul." You will neutralize it immediately. Your emotions are compulsive.

A man said to me, "I'm not jealous. I don't have a jealous bone in my body." But actually the opposite was true. He had employed detectives, checking up every day on his fiancée. She discovered it and broke off the engagement and would have nothing more to do with him.

Oftentimes I say to women, "Don't pay too much attention to what a man says. Watch what he does. What he does is what he means."

His actions belied his statement that there was not a jealous bone in his body. I explained to him that jealousy cripples him emotionally and blocks all his good, holding him back in all phases of his life. Jealousy is the green-eyed monster. He began to see that his jealousy was abnormal and was really based on a sense of inferiority and inadequacy within himself. Jealousy is a child of fear. Love casts out fear, for fear is a torment; and jealousy burns up the tissues like a consuming fire.

If a man loves a woman, he does not do anything unloving. He trusts her in the same manner as, when a child, he looked into his mother's eyes and saw love there. If a man loves a woman, he loves to see her as she ought to be: happy, joyous, free, and expressing herself at her highest level. Love is not jealousy. Love is not possessiveness. Love is not suspicion, neither is it emotional blackmail, such as, "If you loved me you would give up smoking or eating ham" or some other similar foolish, asinine statement. Love has nothing to do with smoking, eating ham or taking a cocktail. Love frees; it gives; it is the Spirit of God in action.

This man learned to pray for a wife, realizing that he marries character and that he doesn't get what he wants in life; he gets what he has established in his mentality. In other words, he must establish the mental equivalent in his subconscious in order to demonstrate what he wants.

Accordingly, he affirmed night and morning: "Infinite Spirit attracts to me a spiritually minded woman who harmonizes with me perfectly. This takes place in Divine order through Divine love. There are mutual love, freedom and respect between us."

He attracted a wonderful legal secretary, and they harmonize perfectly. Every time he thinks of her, he affirms: "God loves you and cares for you." There is no occasion for jealousy where love dwells. He realizes that it is impossible to think of two things at the same time. He can't think of jealousy and love at the same time; no more so than he could laugh and cry at the same time. Two unlike things repel each other. Love and jealousy cannot dwell together.

Jealousy Is a Mental Poison

A jealous person usually blames others as if they were responsible for his inferiority or inadequacy. A jealous person generates mental poisons which bring on all manner of disease. Actually, he is destroying himself from the inside. Remember, you are unique. There is no one in all the world like you. Others do not have the same toe-print or thumbprint; neither do they have the same digestive or glandular systems. They don't think, speak or act like you.

You are an individualized expression of God, and you are here to express yourself in a new and wonderful way. There is no misfit in the universe. You are needed. There is no unwanted note in the symphony; all notes are necessary. "We are all parts of one stupendous whole, whose body nature is and God the soul."

To be envious of others is to demean yourself. It means you are rejecting your own Divinity, which is the Source of all blessings. When jealous of another, you are placing that person on a pedestal and demoting yourself, thereby attracting lack, loss, limitation and impoverishment to yourself. It makes no sense. You have heard the expression, "She is green with envy." This is why jealousy is called the green-eyed monster. The eyes are the windows of the soul. It is true the eyes reveal jealousy, which is a mental sickness. Remember also, a jealous person is an angry person.

Though while he lived he blessed his soul: and men will praise thee, when thou doest well to thyself (Psalms 49:18). Do the very best you can, radiating love and goodwill to all. Love is cordiality, geniality, kindness, good feeling toward all, wishing for everyone all the blessings of life. Love is the fulfilling of the law of health, wealth, peace and prosperity. Cooperate with others. Become enthusiastic. Claim that you are always expressing yourself at the highest level. As you continue in this attitude of mind, you will receive approbation, promotion and recognition.

Learn to Sell Yourself

You can always sell faith, confidence, laughter, goodwill, zeal and enthusiasm; furthermore, these qualities are translatable to abundance, security, true expression and a full life. Rejoice in the affluence of others. As you do, you will attract more wealth to yourself. To be jealous or envious of the wealth of others is to impoverish yourself all the more. Actually, you are denying your own Divinity and saying to yourself: "They can have all that good and I can't," thereby depriving yourself of the very things you seek. Envy and jealousy represent gross ignorance. Ignorance is the only sin, and all the suffering in the world is the consequence.

Sons of God

For as many as are led by the Spirit of God, they are the sons of God (Romans 8:14). You are a son, or expression, of God when you begin to express health, vitality, beauty, love and success in your life. What governs you now? Are you governed by wisdom, truth and beauty, or by ignorance, fear and superstition? The dominant mood governs you. Let the Spirit of light, love, truth and joy rule and govern you, and you will begin to express more and more of the attributes and qualities of God.

Learn to Lead a Full and Happy Life

Saturate your mind with these truths: "At the center of my being is peace. God's river of peace saturates my whole being. I am Divinely guided in all ways. Divine love dissolves everything unlike itself in my subconscious mind. I salute the Divinity in every person I meet, and I make it a habit to call forth the Divinity in every person by silently affirming, 'God's love fills your soul.' I realize that God is personified in all men and women. God flows through me now, filling up all the empty vessels in my life. God's riches—spiritual, mental and material—flow through me now, and I am immersed in the Holy Omnipresence. Wonders happen as I pray."

12

A New Look at Reincarnation

God is the Eternal Now! Timeless, spaceless, ageless, and without face, form or figure, the Living Spirit Almighty within man. In this chapter, the author is not dealing with time and space theories, however, though he certainly has no quarrel with those who differ with this presentation. I believe the time has come in the field of mental and spiritual laws and in our thinking and practice to make a clear-cut decision as to what to do with the misunderstood subject of reincarnation, which is believed by great numbers of people in many parts of the world.

The highest light in the theory of reincarnation is melioristic; i.e., man is becoming better by the slow, external process of coming back again and again through the womb of a woman until such time as he becomes perfect and then returns no more. Nothing is done in this unconscious process, rooted in mere habit transmission, about the ringing challenge: *Be ye therefore perfect, even as your Father which is in heaven is perfect* (Matthew 5:48).

Be ye means ye are, i.e., spiritually perfect, for the Reality of every person is the Spirit (God) within. We must not surrender to a racial error perpetuated by the pronouncement of those who fail to see that we are not victims of the past and that the Timeless One is within us. *A new beginning is a new end. I am Alpha and Omega . . . saith the Lord . . .* (Revelation 1:8). Let us put on the garment of wisdom, truth and beauty instead of the menial garments of "poor man, sick man, beggar man, thief through the weary cycles of time-space forms of reference.

Einstein has brought us to the gate of the Temple Beautiful by toppling the false gods of time and space, and revealing that time has no existence apart from your mind or consciousness. Time is a state of mind; it is your relationship to events. Time is a series of events in a unitary wholeness. It is said that Einstein explained relativity by saying: "If you converse with a beautiful girl for an hour, it seems like a minute. If you sit on a hot stove for a minute, it seems like an hour." Time is psychological, the way you think and feel. We are not referring to the sun time, based on the motion of the earth around the sun.

From the Book of Luke

And he began to say unto them, This day is this scripture fulfilled in your ears (Luke 4:21). In those days they were waiting for the Messiah to come, but the Messiah is within you—the God Presence. It was never born and it will never die. It is instantly available to you. Peace is now, harmony is now, love is now, joy is now, beauty is now, power is now, illumination is now, inspiration is now, the healing power is now. All these factors are of God, and you might as well take and claim all these now rather than fifty years from now. Your Savior is within you—the Presence of God—the only Presence, Power, Cause and Substance.

Let God Arise in You

Let us begin to strip ourselves of all disguises and tune in with the Infinite, while claiming that what is true of God is true of us. This means, essentially, the willful cessation of the automatic, weary round of rebirths on the three-dimensional plane, refreshing ourselves in the menial garments of the slave to carnal, materialistic thinking and living.

The scientific spiritual thinker looks at the theory of reincarnation from a new standpoint altogether. The scientific thinker starts with "the Pattern on the Mount," wherein man is one with God. We must cease trying to become the illumined and God-like man based on the slow-paced belief of millions who have placed themselves in the Procrustean bed of karma and reincarnation to arise retailored in garments ill befitting a son of the Infinite and a child of Eternity.

All of us should wear the proper garment (mood, feeling), which is the royal, seamless robe; otherwise, we will remain in the darkness of spiritual ignorance. If all your thoughts were loving, peaceful and harmonious all day long, your body would become so rarefied and attenuated that the molecular vibrations of your body would be invisible, yet you would be here. Your loved ones are all around you, separated by frequency only.

The Law of Life Is the Law of Belief

By believing in the theory of reincarnation or countless cycles of rebirth on this earth, you drift from safe mooring and fall from spiritual grace. Your subconscious belief in cycles of fleshly rebirth to expiate or atone for sins, errors or crimes in past lives holds you in spiritual bondage and thralldom and indicates a guilt complex. All this results in self punishment, since the Spirit or Life Principle (God) in you does not condemn or punish. All judgment is given to the son, which is your mind. *Thou art of purer eyes than to behold evil, and canst not look on iniquity* . . . (Habakkuk 1:13).

Begin now to put out all karmic, purgatorial fires by true faith and conviction in God's love and beauty here and now, and press on to the virgin's fields of truth and beauty. You must not be deterred by a mirage of mere meliorism. Refuse to be satisfied by anything but the promised land of Spiritual Reality.

The Wine of Spiritual Wisdom

In *materia medica* circles it is customary to discard the textbooks of yesterday's pathologies and nostrums. Likewise, you must discard the old garments of "sick man, poor man," etc. and arrive at the hour of decision in your own mind where the best wine of spiritual wisdom shall be put forth for the guests who hunger for a more wholesome fare.

The new nuclear physics, with great courage and faith, has also, without hesitation, discarded the gross atomistic concept of yesterday. They have demonstrated their own miracle, such as nuclear transubstantiation, time-space fusion, television, radio, space travel, inter-atomic energy, etc. Science is also beginning to kneel and pray before the Altar of Being.

By laboring in the vineyard of your own mind, you, too, can bring forth better fruit. Open your mind and heart to the influx of the Holy Spirit. All unworthy concepts must go into the limbo of spiritual ignorance; foremost among these stands this well-regarded theory of reincarnation, whereby mole-like progress is decreed by age-old, earth- bound thinking.

When Jesus said . . . *The kingdom of God cometh not with observation. Neither shall they say, Lo here! or, lo there! for, behold, the kingdom of God is within you* (Luke 17:20-21), was he not anticipating the relativity of time-space concepts? When he declared: . . . *Behold, now is the accepted time; behold, now is the day of salvation* (II Corinthians 6:2), *Say not ye, There are yet four months, and then cometh harvest? behold, I say unto you, Lift up your eyes, and look on the fields; for they are white already to harvest* (John 4:35), and . . . *Before Abraham was, I am* (John 8:58), was he not collapsing time and space in this 'business' of soul-saving and man-redeeming from the thralldom of erroneous Oriental and Occidental beliefs?

Jesus demonstrated instant resurrection, thereby short circuiting all reincarnation lagging on the way to the promised land of spiritual realization . . . *Today shalt thou be with me in paradise* (Luke 23:43), not tomorrow, next week or next year, for in His eyes time is not.

Free yourself mentally from the self-imposed, psychologically imprisoning embodiment. Become a son of God and leap for joy beneath the morning stars of light, love, truth and beauty, which are timeless and ageless and light up the heavens of your own mind.

True Incarnation

Leave all the lesser altars and idols and commune with the indwelling God with clean hands and a pure heart. *Unto the pure all things are pure* . . . (Titus 1:15). Every time you pray and appropriate more of Divinity, you have been reincarnated, spiritually speaking. True reincarnation is the birth of God in your mind and heart, whereby you becomes seized with a Divine frenzy and you become God-intoxicated. This does not mean that you have to be reborn on this earth or planet. The word "earth" means much more than this particular world. Earth in the *I Ching* and in biblical symbology means manifestation, which also means that you can manifest and experience a greater measure of Divinity in the next dimension of life, where you go every night of your life, and which men in their ignorance call you dead. How could God die? God is the Living Spirit within you.

In the Hindu scripture it says: "Spirit was never born and will never die; water wets it not, fire burns it not, wind blows it not away." Why, therefore, would you grieve for your loved ones in the next dimension? Life is growth, expansion, newness. Their journey is ever onward, upward and Godward. They go from glory to glory, from strength to strength, and from wisdom to a greater wisdom, for there is no end to the glory which is man.

What is true on one plane of life is true on all planes, and your loved ones in the next dimension grow, learn and expand in wisdom. There are teachers there as well as here. Actually, our loved ones are all around us, though separated by rates of vibration. This is a world of densities, frequencies and intensities. The child whose life, perhaps, was snuffed out in the womb still lives forever and is a grace note in the symphony of all creation. In a grand symphony, grace notes are just as important as the somber tones. The child grows, expands, unfolds and listens to the entire symphony and has a subjective access to all loved ones on this plane as well as on the next, who, through love, are welded into the great symphony called the music of the spheres.

Jesus, Moses, Buddha, Paul and other illumined seers are the great conductors who lead all of us in the grand symphony of all creation.

You Are Not a Victim of Karma

Karma is generally referred to as the force generated by a person's action that is held in Hinduism and Buddhism to be the motive power for the round of rebirths and deaths endured by him until he has achieved spiritual liberation and freed himself from the effects of such force. Look at it in a simple way: It is the law of action and reaction, of sowing and reaping. Whatever is impressed on the subconscious mind is expressed as experiences, events, circumstances and conditions. When you learn the laws of mind, you are no longer a victim but a victor.

There is no time or space in the mind-principle; therefore, you can at this very moment begin to feed your subconscious mind with life-giving patterns of harmony, wholeness, beauty, joy, love and goodwill to all, and there will be an automatic response from your subconscious in accordance with your spiritual, habitual thinking and imagery. Think of a pail of dirty, filthy water and pour distilled water into it, even drop by drop. If you have the patience, you eventually will have clear, pure water which you can drink.

Likewise, you can clean out the Augean stable even though it was dirty for forty years right now. It doesn't make any difference to the water hose you use whether the stable was dirty yesterday or fifty years ago. Likewise, when you pour into your subconscious the waters of life, wonders will happen in your life. Take time out morning and evening and affirm feelingly, knowingly and joyously: "The Infinite oceans of life, love, joy, truth and beauty are flowing through me harmoniously and peacefully, vitalizing, cleansing, healing and transforming my whole being. The wholeness and peace of God reign supreme in my mind and heart; I am cleansed and I sing the song of the jubilant soul."

As you saturate your subconscious with these truths, you will gradually obliterate and expunge from your deeper mind all the negative patterns. Prayer changes things in the sense that it changes the person who prays. No matter what the problem is or how difficult it seems, it is due to a group of negative thoughts and emotions lodged in your subjective depths. By filling your mind with the truths of God (namely, the eternal verities) you crowd out and neutralize everything unlike God.

Suppose you misused the principles of mathematics for twenty years, which, perhaps, caused you a lot of trouble and financial losses, and let us assume you learned how to add, subtract, multiply, etc. Surely you realize that the principles of mathematics have nothing against you. The minute you begin to use them the right way, there is an automatic response. The engineer building a bridge has to conform to the principles of mathematics. He learns all about stress and strains. When he builds the bridge, that is a prayer, because he conforms to a universal principle which existed before man walked the earth.

If you misuse the principles and laws of chemistry, you will get into a lot of trouble, but when you learn about valence, laws of attraction, repulsion, atomic weights, etc., you can bring forth marvelous compounds which will bless humanity. Your common sense tells you that the principles of chemistry hold no grudge against you because you did not use them in the right way previously.

Your mind is also a principle. When you think good, good follows; when you think negatively, negation and misery follow. Karma, or the law of action and reaction, is inexorable only as long as we do not pray. A new beginning is a new end. *I am Alpha and Omega, the beginning and end . . .* (Revelation 22:13).

Changed Attitudes Change Everything

. . . *Be ye transformed by the renewing of your mind* . . . (Romans 12:2). The late Ernest Holmes, author of *Science of Mind*, told me that he studied with Emma Curtis Hopkins, who once told him of a wonderful event recorded in the archives of a state penal institution. This is the essence of it: A man was sentenced over seventy years ago to be hanged. During the interim between his sentence and its time of fulfillment, he became aware of the love and the truth about God. In a pamphlet given him, he learned that God was the "bad man's deliverer." *Thou art of purer eyes than to behold evil, and canst not look on iniquity* . . . (Habakkuk 1:13).

God does not condemn, judge or punish. You punish yourself by misuse of law. This murderer looked to God and His love and contemplated the wonders of it all. It is said he sought the face of the all-good. When I look at your face I recognize you. God has no face, form or figure. God is Spirit. It means he recognized the great truth: *For the Lord is good; his mercy is everlasting; and his truth endureth to all generations* (Psalm 100:5).

This man had actually committed the murder for which he was sentenced. To the great confusion and perplexity of the officers of the law, when the man was led to the gallows, the platform, which would ordinarily tip at the slightest weight, became firm when the condemned man stepped upon it. They tried again and again to no avail, until, finally, he was given his freedom.

Did not the efficacy of his High Watch (which means his veneration and adoration of the Divine Presence) plus the transformation of his heart halt the so-called Karma of the ordinarily mandated treadmill of cause and effect and enable this murderer to step off into a new order of emancipated consciousness and experience? The love of God indeed surpasses all understanding, and it does illumine the path we tread. The wonders and blessings of God know no ending.

Karma, or reaping what you have sown, turns out to be inflexible and inexorable only as long as you do not pray or meditate on the truths of God. Mere reading of affirmations and perfunctory prayer will not change matters, however. *Blessed are they which do hunger and thirst after righteousness: for they shall be filled* (Matthew 5:6).

An intense desire to become a new man in God and filling your mind with the great truths of God enables you to become a transformed man; and since the law of your subconscious is compulsive, you are compelled to express your inner assumptions and beliefs, and you no longer can repeat the previous errors. You rise above karma, and the unpleasant consequences of past mistakes are wiped out. No matter how awful the crime—be it murder or any other heinous offense—it can be expunged from the mind when you rise high enough in consciousness.

Remember, it is the deep hunger and thirst of your heart for Di vine love and grace, plus a deep desire to become the new man in God, that is essential to wipe out the punishment that must otherwise follow negative and destructive thinking. Paul, for example, who sent many people to death, experienced an inner illumination and became a transformed man. *And God wrought special miracles by the hands of Paul* (Acts 19:11) . . . *This one thing I do, forgetting those things which are behind, and reaching forth unto those things which are before, I press toward the mark for the prize* . . . (Philippians 3:13-14). The prize is health, happiness, peace, inspiration and oneness with the Divinity that shapes your ends.

The Nature of Your Belief

To believe (which means to accept something as true) that God is punishing you for the mistakes of the past is to have a false concept of God. Whatever concept you hold of God has its effect on your life. If you have a false, superstitious concept of God, there will be chaos and confusion in your life. Ask yourself: "What do I really believe as true about the Infinite Presence within me?" Your answer is the most important thing in your life. It must come from the heart. It is not adequate to say: "I believe in God." What kind of God do you believe in?

For example, begin to believe that God is omnipotent and all wise and possesses boundless love, infinite intelligence, infinite perfection, and absolute harmony, and that what is true of God must, therefore, be true of you, for God, or Infinite Spirit, indwells you and is the Reality of you. God is man made manifest. Spirit and form are one. God is life, and life and its manifestation are one.

Begin to believe in your heart that God is all love, intelligence, truth and beauty and is your Higher Self in the same way as you believe that you are alive. Then everything in your life will change. All the departments of your life will begin to improve, such as your health, wealth, love and expression. You will go from glory to glory, and your good will multiply exceedingly. The day will break for you and all the shadows will flee away.

The Opiate of the People

To believe that it is essential for you to come back again and again in order to work out some karma or to suffer for past misdeeds in a former life is a sort of an opiate. It dulls the mind. It is a form of alibi which acts as an anesthetic and prevents spiritual unfoldment. You must see the foolishness of such a belief. It is a complete contradiction of the teachings of the Bible and the ageless wisdom.

In the ninth chapter of John, which is a mystical book, you read about a blind man being instantly healed by Jesus. *And his disciples asked Mm, saying, Master, who did sin, this man, or his parents, that he was born blind? Jesus answered, Neither hath this man sinned, nor his parents: but that the works of God should be made manifest in him* (John 9:2-3). The works of God represent the law of cause and effect.

He brushed aside all the prevalent beliefs at that time, such as, that he must have been a sinner in a former life or that the sins of his parents were visited on him. *And it was the Sabbath day when Jesus made the clay, and opened his eyes* (John 9:14). The Sabbath day has nothing to do with days of the week. It means your conviction, the point of complete mental acceptance; then your prayer is answered.

The only loss, limitation, restriction or evil in the world is our belief in loss, our belief in limitation, our belief in restriction and our belief in evil or disease. This is known as the "son of perdition" or sense of loss spoken of in the Bible. *Come now, and let us reason together, saith the Lord: though your sins be as scarlet, they shall be as white as snow; though they be red like crimson, they shall be as wool* (Isaiah 1:18).

The ninth chapter of John is the answer to those who are always asking the question: Why is an innocent child born deaf, lame or crippled? The law of cause and effect is a changeless principle. You may consciously use the law. If you have been misusing or misdirecting the law, you can reverse your mental attitude; then you will change the sequence of events. *I form the light, and create darkness: I make peace, and create evil: I the Lord do all these things* (Isaiah 45:7). This means you can use the law two ways. When you use the law wisely and constructively, men call it God, or good. When you use the law negatively, maliciously, ignorantly or stupidly, men call it evil, because we inflict all manner of suffering upon ourselves by misdirecting the law of life.

Our feelings and moods create. What tone do you strike during the creative act? For example, if there is someone in the parents' world whom they hate the sight of, or if there is a voice that they resent or detest, or if they are drunk or under the influence of narcotics and during the creative act the ovum happens to be fertilized, there is a corresponding expression brought forth. These are the blind and deaf states of consciousness from which blind and deaf children come forth. Whatever tone is struck by the parents, a corresponding expression comes forth by the law of reciprocal relationship. The child is not a victim of heredity in the true sense of the term. The child that is born is a victim of the mood of the parents during coition.

In Ezekiel it is written: *What mean ye, that ye use this proverb concerning the land of Israel, saying, The fathers have eaten sour grapes, and the children's teeth are set on edge? As I live, saith the Lord God, ye shall not have occasion any more to use this proverb in Israel* (Ezekial 18:2-3). The only thing passed on to children are the moods, mental states or beliefs of the parents. It is possible, for in- stance, for anyone to have a son who may become a Shakespeare, Beethoven, Lincoln or Paderewski, particularly if they are constantly dwelling on the characteristics of any of these personalities at the moment of conception.

I knew a blind couple in New York City who gave birth to a wonderful boy. He became an outstanding doctor and an illumined man. I was acquainted also with a tubercular father and mother in the Bronx area of New York who gave birth to a wonderful girl who has since become a great musician and the mother of two lovely children.

If you are lifted up in consciousness to the point of acceptance or belief that your son will be a noble, dignified, spiritual minded man, then according to the law of reciprocal relationship, a corresponding mood or quality of the Infinite will come forth.

The sins of the fathers are the fears, superstitions, false beliefs and anxieties which disturb the children. These moods and mental states are transmitted to the children and disturb them mentally and physically. Sins are mistakes of the mind, or misuse of the law. We sin when we miss the mark of harmony, health and peace. The bad and evil acts of parents or grandparents can only be transmitted through the mind. In this way, the superstitions, fears and the errors of the past generation are given to the present.

By illustration, a father instills fear of God by depicting a picture of a punitive Deity who will punish him. The son grows up believing in a God of wrath, a sort of despot living in the skies, ruling the world according to His whims and caprice.

Realizing Your Freedom

As you begin to realize the Omnipotence of the Spirit within and the power of your own thought, you cease giving power to anything else. You enthrone the concepts of freedom, peace, joy and wholeness in your mind, and you live with these ideas, entering into the reality of them. In other words, you sense and feel that you are a son of God, and heir to all the qualities, powers and attributes of God. You declare your freedom and write your declaration of independence and freedom in your heart. Begin to love all things good; the law of your mind will respond accordingly by opening for you the windows of heaven and pouring out a blessing that there is not room enough to receive.

The Law of Averages

The late Judge Thomas Troward in his inimitable books on mental and spiritual laws pointed out that all of us are immersed in the mass mind or, as he termed it, the law of averages or race mind. Today there are about four billion people thinking into that one mind, and if we do not do our own thinking, the mass mind will do it for us. We must, therefore, pray ourselves out of that mass mind.

Jesus did not say to the blind man, "You must expiate for your karma." No, he healed him instantaneously, for the Infinite Presence condemns no one, and though a man is a cripple, he can be healed; if he is deaf, he can hear. Blind people have been healed at Lourdes and other such shrines.

Another Mozart Can Be Born

All the great men and women who ever lived on this plane still live and they have left their accomplishments, experiences and achievements as impressions in the universal subjective mind. We read of their works in history, song and prose. A man's son, psychologically speaking, is his idea or feeling about anything. He can give conception to any state he is capable of conceiving. If a man, therefore, admires or dwells on the qualities and attributes of

Mozart and is intensely interested in his musical accomplishments and would love to give birth to a son possessing similar accomplishments, "as within, so without." During the creative act a Mozart-like character would result and would undoubtedly be another Mozart in the musical field, but it would not be the personality called Mozart being reincarnated.

Dictators, Despots and Tyrants

Dictators and despots are extensions in space of the dictator complex present in the context of the race mind. By changing ourselves we change the world. The world consists of ourselves in aggregation. When a cruel dictator appears in the world, it does not mean he is a new incarnation of Genghis Khan or any other dictator or tyrant who lived before.

Boys and girls learn about the wars in school and in the home in which their country was involved; and, in some instances, they are taught to hate the neighboring nations. These children grow up with resentment and rage at the wrongs committed by these men. They read avidly of the crimes, atrocities and acts of violence. These states are impressed on their subconscious minds. All of these moods, feelings and thoughts which are entertained become objectified as conditions, experiences and events. Whatever is impressed on the subconscious must be expressed in the world.

The tyrant who appears in a nation is the embodiment of the state of consciousness of the people in the particular country, nation or whatever part of the world in which he may appear. It is never a man who lived a thousand or two thousand years ago who is being reborn. It is a state of consciousness that is born again.

Hear the Words of the Psalmist

I have been young, and now am old; yet have I not seen the righteous forsaken, nor his seed begging bread (Psalm 37:25). "I was young," meaning I did not understand the laws of mind; "now am old"—age, biblically speaking, means the dawn of wisdom. When you are spiritually wise and understand the way your mind works, then the righteous (right use of the laws of Life) are never forsaken. You are righteous when you think right, feel right, act right and do right according to the Golden Rule and the law of love, or goodwill, to all.

If parents and teachers would teach the laws of mind and the eternal verities to the young, their seed would never beg bread. This means these children shall never become the beggars, outcasts, thieves and tyrants of the world. In other words, your children will fulfill your conviction of them. Children grow up in the image and likeness of the dominant mental, emotional and spiritual climate supplied by the home.

By teaching the youth of the nation who they really are, and by showing them the way, the truth and the light, we can build a heaven on earth and prevent the appearance in the world of dictators, despots, tyrants and undesirable states of consciousness which are perpetuated by prejudices, racial hatreds and fear of the unknown. Teach children of the great accomplishments of the poets, artists, engineers, chemists, physicists, astronomers, mystics and the illumined seers of the ages, and boys and girls will tend to emulate the ideals portrayed.

Awakening from the Dream of Limitation

There are many cases of men and women who have completely lost their former identity and personality, who have assumed new lives, entered different professions, and, in many cases, remarried. These people were victims of amnesia, or loss of memory concerning their former selves. They could not remember their former husbands or wives and children. They had no recollection of their former professions or occupations. They assumed a new role in life. They were changed entirely because they had changed their consciousness.

In the spiritual sense we are all victims of amnesia. We have forgotten who we really are, and we tell ourselves that we are worms of the dust. Take, for example, a man who awakens from sleep and has completely forgotten who he is. He gravitates to the slums. His friends, knowing what has happened, try to coax him back to his former state. Because of amnesia, his former way of life is completely blotted from his memory. He believes his place is in the slums. He only smiles at these old acquaintances and former friends whom he no longer knows. He accepts his present role. The day finally comes when his memory is suddenly restored and he awakens to his rightful status. With certainty and promptness, he returns to his environment consonant with the dignity of his upbringing. He wonders why he is in the slums. What has transpired is like a dream to him.

The One Appearing in the Many

Your life on this plane is like the several stanzas of a poem or scenes of a play, because it is the One Being dramatizing Himself as the many. Ancient wisdom teaches that illumination, or the great awakening to your Divinity, can happen here and now. The old aphorism states: "If it be not now, yet it will come; the readiness is all."

In order to elucidate this point, take a solid metallic substance and heat it. The temperature rises, but for awhile it appears that no change is taking place. However, the moment the degree of heat is reached which denotes its melting point, it begins to liquefy, thus changing its shape and, seemingly, its nature also. Likewise, water can be turned into steam, which is invisible, since pure steam cannot be seen. Water also becomes snow, ice and hail. All are different rates of vibration of water.

When a liquid is caused to become a gas, these changes are brought about by an increase in the rapidity of vibration of the constituent particles, whether initially they are solid or liquid. The same law applies to all of us.

You can raise your vibration rate and transform yourself by lifting yourself up to a high state of awareness through the constant contemplation on the Presence and Power of the Infinite. In this meditative, quiet, lovely state, you will gradually appropriate more and more of the attributes and qualities of God. By constantly meditating in this manner, you will find a great expansion of consciousness. It is like the heat that melts the solid. The day will come when you will melt away all inhibitions, fears, false beliefs and doubts and become the God-man here and now. This change may come, as it did in the case of Paul, in the twinkling of an eye, like the volatilization of a liquid into a gas.

The Power Within You

The power within man is capable of nullifying all false beliefs and man-made laws. Cases are reported where cripples invalided for years leap and run in the presence of fires. In emergencies, mothers and wives lift automobiles to extricate their children and husbands. Where is this power? It is within them. Fires and emergencies are not needed to stir up the God-Presence within. Man can resurrect this power and wisdom by silent contemplation in the silence of his own soul. Truth is lived in the silence; Truth is heard in the silence; Truth is transmitted in the silence; for God abides in the silence.

When you unite with the Infinite, you are in union with that which is beyond time and space. Then you are free of that which has taken place in time and space. In other words, you go from time to Eternity and find the peace that passeth all understanding.

13

Words of Wisdom

And a certain woman, which had an issue of blood twelve years, and had suffered many things of many physicians, and had spent all that she had, and was nothing bettered, but rather grew worse, When she had heard of Jesus, came in the press behind, and touched his garment. For she said, if I may touch but his clothes, I shall be whole. And straightway the fountain of her blood was dried up; and she felt in her body that she was healed of that plague. And Jesus, immediately knowing in himself that virtue had gone out of him, turned him about in the press, and said, Who touched my clothes? And his disciples said unto him, Thou seest the multitude thronging thee, and sayest thou, Who touched me? And he looked round about to see her that had done this thing. But the woman fearing and trembling, knowing what was done in her, came and fell down before him, and told him all the truth. And he said unto her, Daughter, thy faith hath made thee whole; go in peace, and be whole of thy plague.

While he yet spake, there came from the ruler of the synagogue's house certain which said, Thy daughter is dead: why troublest thou the Master any further? As soon as Jesus heard the word that was spoken, he saith unto the ruler of the synagogue, Be not afraid, only believe. And he suffered no man to follow him, save Peter, and James, and John the brother of James. And he cometh to the house of the ruler of the synagogue, and seeth the tumult, and them that wept and wailed greatly. And when he was come in, he saith unto them, Why make ye this ado, and weep? the damsel is not dead, but sleepeth. And they laughed him to scorn. But when he had put them all out, he taketh the father and the mother of the damsel, and them that were with him, and entereth in where the damsel was lying. And he took the damsel by the hand, and said unto her, Talitha cumi; which is, being interpreted, Damsel, I say unto thee, arise. And straightway the damsel arose, and walked; for she was of the age of twelve years. And they were astonished with a great astonishment. And he charged them straightly that no man should know it; and commanded that something should be given her to eat (Mark 5:25-43).

All the stories in the Bible unfold in the mind of the individual. One of the inner meanings of the word *Jesus* is illumined reason. When you are in tune with the Infinite and your mind is healed of its limitations and false beliefs, then you are this Presence personified as Jesus, the Power that can resurrect the dead hopes of man.

You are the woman with the issue of blood for the simple reason that a running womb is not a productive or creative womb. In other words, she was incapable of conceiving for twelve years and could not give form to the longing of her heart because of the running of the issue of blood. It is said her faith closed the womb and healed her. As the womb closes, it can give form to the idea or seed.

When you cleanse your mind of fear, hostility, resentment and self-condemnation and fill your mind with Divine love and the spirit of forgiveness toward all, you can then assume that you are one with your ideal or desire and remain faithful to that assumption. You will then succeed in resurrecting your child (your desire). Walk in the feeling that you now are what you long to be, and your assumption will crystallize in your subconscious and come to pass.

The child or damsel spoken of in the Bible means that the cherished desire of your heart is considered dead until you awaken it, nourish and sustain it with faith and confidence and make it visible on the screen of space. Your assumption, when sustained by you, invariably resurrects what you affirm to be true. When you pray, you close the door of your senses, rejecting the evidence of the five senses, and live in the bold assertion that you are that which your senses deny. Your senses challenge you and mock you.

That is why verse 40 says: *They laughed him to scorn.* This means the thoughts in your own mind which challenge you are based on the beliefs of the mass mind and try to dissuade you from believing in the One Power. Reject the evidence of your senses which mock your assumption, and you take the father and mother of the child into your mind, which means your I AMness. This is the Father and Mother of all creation, your Awareness, or Consciousness. As you claim and feel you now are what you long to be, the condition which you desired and assumed to be true becomes objectified in your world and bears witness to your inner conviction.

Looking in the Mirror

We cannot destroy our image or change our estimate of ourselves by looking in the mirror. We must be aware of the law of mind, which states that we become what we contemplate. It is the nature of love, as it is also the nature of hatred, to change us into the image and likeness of that which we contemplate. When we study the wars and revolutions as portrayed in history, we discover that in many instances when men killed the tyrants and despots of the world, which represented to them arrogance and greed, they themselves became that which they thought they had destroyed.

This is obvious in some of the countries of the world today. Hate betrays man and condemns him to be that which he condemns. Oftentimes the conqueror becomes like the conquered foe. A nation is an aggregation of individuals, and if you study the people in any nation, they act towards others in the way they act toward each other. For example, if a country has enslaved its people, and it then attacks another country, its purpose is to enslave the population of that country. When we look at a war in which one country wants to dominate the other, you will find that the war is started by those who, within the state, had control and were dominant over the fortunes of the rest.

It is foolish to contemplate something that you heartily dislike, because by condemning it you will become it. Your concept or estimate of yourself is the cause of all conditions and circumstances of your life. All changes must come from within yourself. There will be no changes on the outside until you change within. It is no use blaming others, and it is useless to blame society for your problems and difficulties. Furthermore, it is a waste of time and effort to blame other nations.

There are those people, for example, who blame the weather for the way they feel, all of which is nonsense. They have forgotten the old aphorism: It is always fair weather when good friends get together. You are forever molding your world in harmony with your inner attitudes and beliefs. Remember also that the behavior of others toward you testifies to that which you have conceived yourself to be. Begin to believe that you are a son of the Living God and heir to all of God's riches. Walk the earth knowing the Light of God shines in you, through you and all around you, and men and women will testify to your new state of consciousness.

Nothing Is Lost

While I was with them in the world, I kept them in thy name; those that thou gavest me I have kept, and none of them is lost, but the son of perdition; that the scripture might be fulfilled (John 17:12).

It is impossible for anything to be lost, for the simple reason that nothing can be lost in the Infinite. It cannot even pass away. Energy cannot be destroyed. It can take many forms, but cannot be lost. The little flower that blooms in the desert blooms forever. It is invisible to the three-dimensional focus, but it blooms forever in the larger dimension of your being. That is to say, it can be seen fourth dimensionally.

For example, a good psychic or sensitive can see the house

which was there before you occupied your present house. You might say that the old house was torn down and you put up the new house, but the pattern of the old house still subsists in the next dimension of mind and can be seen by a clairvoyant or good sensitive.

You might say that you have lost health, but wholeness, beauty and perfection can never cease to be. The Infinite Healing Presence was never born and will never die. You, by a descent in consciousness, perhaps due to fear or negative emotion, to a lower level, caused health and vitality to disappear; but all you have to do is to turn your eyes to the Eternal One and identify yourself mentally and spiritually with the Infinite Healing Presence, calling upon It to restore and vivify your whole being, and It will respond to your conviction.

Sanctify Yourself

And for their sakes I sanctify myself, that they also might be sanctified through the truth (John 17:19). Cease trying to change others through effort or mental coercion. The thing to do is to change yourself. Change your concept of the other, for your concept is what you see. In order to change your concept of the other, you do it best by changing your concept of yourself. You must realize that it was your concept of yourself that made you see others as you did. You see others through the contents of your own mentality.

The world you see is the world you are. If you had a noble, dignified, God-like concept of yourself, you would be unable to see the ugly and the unlovely in others. When you look through the eyes of love to your child in the cradle, what do you see there? The answer is simple. Sanctify yourself, and in so doing you sanctify others.

Unto the pure all things are pure . . . (Titus 1:15) . . . *There is nothing unclean of itself: but to him that esteemeth any thing to be unclean, to him it is unclean* (Romans 14:14).

There is nothing in itself unclean, but you, by your concept or estimate of yourself, see others as clean or unclean. It is the most natural thing in the world for a pear tree to bear pears, an apple tree to bear apples, and for you to mold the circumstances of your life in harmony with your inner nature.

I am the vine, ye are the branches . . . (John 15:5). A branch is rooted in the vine. In order to change the fruit you must change the vine. I AM is God, Being, Life, Awareness; and four billion people in the world are rooted in the I AM, or Life Principle. All men and women are extensions of the I AM, or Life Principle; therefore, they are all rooted in you and you in them. Like fruit, others bear witness to the state of consciousness in which you dwell.

Your I AMness, your Consciousness, is the way in which you change your world. Whatever you attach to I AM you become. As you affirm with feeling, I am illumined, inspired, loving, harmonious, peaceful, happy and strong, you will resurrect these qualities that lie dormant within you, and wonders will happen in your life. When men and women help you in the realization of your dreams, they are playing their part and are messengers testifying to your beliefs and convictions. You wrote the play, and other men and women execute the parts conforming to your concept of yourself.

It is wholly unnecessary for you to proselyte and try to make the world holy. You will not change the world that way. You will change the world when you actually become the embodiment of that which you want the world to be. Remember a simple truth: Unless you are that which you want the world to be, you will never see it in this world.

. . . And his name shall be called Wonderful . . . (Isaiah 9:6). Recently a woman gave me a list of all the things she wanted in life: home, car, friends, money, marriage, new position, new apartment, etc. I suggested that she use an age-old prayer technique, which includes them all.

Accordingly, she began to affirm and actually sing to herself: "It is wonderful." She kept repeating this most of the day for about five or six days. She got into a joyous, ecstatic mood and felt wonderful. She didn't ask herself: What is wonderful? To her, the expression meant that God was working wonders in her life, knowing that if she were looking for results she would lose the joyous and happy sensation.

The sequel to her new mood was most interesting. Her boss proposed to her, gave her a diamond ring, bought her a Cadillac car, arranged a marriage date and a trip by air around the world. Everything in her life miraculously changed, and all her dreams were fulfilled. "It is wonderful" includes all things.

Creation Is Finished

. . . *The works were finished from the foundation of the world* (Hebrews 4:3). Many have stated to the author that they have seen events in their dreams before they happened on the screen of space; therefore, they postulated that things were predetermined. In the next dimension of mind, the thought and the event are one, and it is possible to see an event before it happens, but you are not fated to experience it.

You can dwell upon eternal verities and saturate your subconscious mind with life-giving patterns, and a new beginning becomes a new end. You mold your future in harmony with your mental transformation. When you change your concept of yourself, you change your relationship to everything in the world. If you take the words of this page and rearrange them, you can write a different interpretation. You did not create the words; you simply rearranged them and got a different result.

Your dominant conviction about yourself, life, God and the universe determines all the events which you encounter; but the things you encounter and experience on the three-dimensional plane always subsisted in another dimension of mind.

God's work is finished. God, or Infinite Spirit, cannot grow, expand or change, for It is the same yesterday, today and forever.

If we really want to grow spiritually, the thing for us to do is to claim that what is true of the Infinite is true of us, for God indwells all of us. As we claim and feel the Truths of God in our hearts, all our ways will be ways of pleasantness and all our paths will be paths of peace.

The Giants Are Within Us

And it came to pass, when men began to multiply on the face of the earth, and daughters were born unto them, That the sons of God saw the daughters of men that they were fair; and they took them wives of all which they chose (Genesis 6:1-2).

There were giants in the earth in those days; and also after that, when the sons of God came in unto the daughters of men, and they bare children to them, the same became mighty men which were of old, men of renown (Genesis 6:4).

The key to Bible interpretations is to transform the factual and historical accounting into mental, psychic and spiritual processes as they unfold the potentialities of Spirit through the instrumentality of man's mind.

Men means mind centers began to be multiplied upon the earth; i.e., made manifest. Daughters (emotional attachments) were born to them instead of positive sons, or true ideas. The sons (sense knowledge and false beliefs), seeing the daughters of men (fears, doubts, superstitions and false knowledge) that they were fair, took to them wives of all which they chose (married or mated on the basis of negative emotional conditioning). As a result of this wrong mating of beliefs (sons) and emotions (daughters), giants were upon the earth in those days (troubles, wars, sickness, etc. appear as the unholy spawn of these unholy marriages).

In this light, Genesis should be interpreted in such a manner that it will reveal to you how you create your own world. Spirit is God. Your state of mind is the sum total of your beliefs, acceptances, conscious and subconscious. But you can change your mind to conform to the eternal truths, which are the same yesterday, today and forever. You can use your mind wisely or unwisely, because of your free will. Everything will change in your life when you let the spirit of goodness, truth and beauty govern your mind.

Beyond the Senses

When your senses are awakened and you become clairvoyant, you will perceive that the earth on which you walk, the air you breathe, and the water you drink, as well as the five elements, are peopled by entities unknown to many but well known to many sensitive and illumined souls.

The Trinity Is Spirit, Mind and Body

Look upon your mind as the medium between Spirit (God) and your body, effecting the passage of Spirit through mind into manifestation. Another way of explaining it is thought, feeling and manifestation.

Implied Phallic Laws

When men (mind) began to be multiplied upon the earth and daughters were born to them. The implied phallic symbolism simply indicates the universal law of action and reaction, as noted in the interplay of idea and emotion, male and female, Adam and Eve. Curiously, it must be noted that woman (emotion, feeling nature) at first did come out of man (Adam, conscious mind, intellect, idea)—a true mating of true man with true emotion (Eve). But after this instance, "daughters were born" to men, as they misdated to negative emotional patterns dictated by the false beliefs of the world, forgetful of the Spirit of God.

Your intellect, when unenlightened by the Spirit, is useful in gathering all kinds of knowledge. It creates terminology such as psychiatry, psychosomatic medicine, Oedipus complex, Electra complex, projective escapism, flight from reality, etc. The average man is covered by a mist and a fog, and the light (intelligence) in him becomes darkness. Fears arise (daughters), and man's unenlightened mind foolishly marries them, until his offspring are as veritable "giants" (troubles, disease, complexes, wars, etc.) in the land (his world of experience).

The Answer

The answer is to align ourselves with the Infinite and let the love, the light and the harmony of the Infinite Healing Presence flow through us regularly, thereby cleansing our subconscious of these negative patterns.

The Sons of Spirit (Ideas of God; Truths of Life)

And God saw that the wickedness of man was great in the earth, and that every imagination of the thoughts of his heart was only evil continually (Genesis 6:5).

This is a rather accurate description of what is really the social picture of the contemporary scene. Fear of disease is rampant on every level, the pornographers' cesspool of iniquity is spreading in all the major cities, and hospitals of all types are rapidly being filled with people mentally and physically ill. We are reading constantly about insecurity, insanity and instability of large numbers of men and women.

Giants are the fearful mismating with the daughters (emotion) of men (intellect). We should find true mating of God's ideas with lovelier daughters (Divine love and Divine beauty) and the joy of the Lord, which is our strength.

Your Constructive Desire

Every constructive desire is a "son of God," an offspring of the Father of Life. This son, or desire, seeks a true mating to be found on spiritual levels only. The desire is good and very good and will bless humanity. As man affirms and believes that the Spirit of God will open up the door for the fulfillment of his desire, he is having a true mental marriage and will be blessed with lovely offspring. The offspring of the Spirit of God moving on the waters of your mind are wisdom, health, peace, prosperity and happiness.

Realize that God in the midst of you is able to close the mouths of lions (disease, death, insecurity, etc.); and wonders will happen as you pray in this manner.

14

The Law of Security

When ye go, ye shall come unto a people secure, and to a large land: for God hath given it into your hands; a place where there is no want of any thing that is in the earth (Judges 18:10).

You are secure when you walk in the realization that God indwells you and walks and talks in you. Realize that you are always in the Holy Omnipresence, surrounded by the sacred circle of God's eternal love. As you continue to do this, you will build up an immunity to all harm. Claim, feel and know that you, your family, your possessions and all things appertaining to you are in the secret place of the Most High, watched over by an Overshadowing Presence which watches over you in all your ways. This is the impregnable fortress, invincible and impervious to everything negative.

In the above verse of Judges, it says: *When ye go, ye shall come unto a people secure*, meaning that wherever you travel, Divine love goes before you making straight, joyous and happy the way. A place where there is no want means that the Presence of God is operating in your life. The Presence of God means the presence of harmony, beauty, love, peace, abundance and security.

And thou shall be secure, because there is hope; yea, thou shall dig about thee, and thou shalt take thy rest in safety (Job 11:18).

Hope springs eternal in the human breast. You may dig in the earth and find precious stones, jewels, oil, water and other precious things. When you dig within yourself, you discover a gold mine full of infinite treasures—the precious stones of wisdom, truth, beauty, inspiration, guidance, intuition, and creative ideas which heal, bless, inspire and protect you, enabling you to sleep in peace every night and to wake in joy. Asleep or awake, wherever you are, you realize that Divine love surrounds you, enfolds you and enwraps you.

The Triumph of Principles

Emerson said that nothing can bring you peace but the triumph of principles. When you learn the laws of life and practice them, you will develop a sense of security. There is the universal law of action and reaction: What is impressed on your subconscious is expressed. When you build an airplane, an automobile or a bridge, the engineer conforms to universal principles. The wheels of your car have to be round; otherwise, you are in trouble. You would not navigate a ship except you learned the laws of navigation. Look at the engineer building a bridge. He operates according to the principles of mathematics, calculating the stress and strain of materials used, the load the bridge is supposed to bear, etc. In other words, the man who navigates an airplane learns the laws of navigation and lives by them.

Some years ago, a speaker for Taniguchi, the spiritual leader of about six million people in Tokyo, Japan, told me that when the floods touch certain cities in Japan, the Truth students are never there. They believe that they are always Divinely guided and watched over by an Overshadowing Presence. One of the teachers told me that he had been scheduled to go by boat to another city, but when he arrived at the place to embark he discovered he was one hour late. His watch had stopped. The ship was lost subsequently in a storm. He believed that God was His guide and protector, watching over him in all ways. His prayer was: God is guiding me and watches over me at all times.

Finding Security Within

Today we have Social Security—pension systems, food stamps, medical care—and billions of dollars are poured out by the Government all over the world to friend and so-called foe; yet there is a deep sense of insecurity, apprehension and fear abroad in the world. In Hollywood and elsewhere we see a pornographic cesspool of iniquity and moral decay, and swingers making a mockery of marriage. People are afraid to go out at night or walk the streets.

Yes, there is a pervading sense of insecurity. Coddling of criminals is quite prevalent. You can write to local legislators and congressmen, for example, telling them how you feel. You can also pray that Infinite Spirit, in Its wisdom, selects men and women for Government positions and for Congressmen who are spiritually dedicated and who have a reverence for things Divine. This will help considerably, and if we had enough people who knew how to pray scientifically, we would have a different Congress.

Venereal disease of all kinds is rampant among young people. Heart disease, cancer and alcoholism are taking their toll. Some say the world is going to the dogs—No, it is going to God. Read the 91st Psalm at night and Psalm 27 in the morning. Saturate your mind with the Truths of God. As you do, you will be a broadcasting station, neutralizing to some degree the toxic effluvia of the mass mind.

I read recently where there is a swing back to the old virtues. One article said young men and women were flocking back to the seminaries and studying the scriptures with an insatiable hunger to serve people. That is a good sign. You don't want to be a part of the mass mind, which means the thinking of four billion people in the world whose thoughts are mostly negative. If you do not do your own thinking, the mass mind moves in upon you and makes a mess of your life.

It is well known that nature abhors extremes. Notice, for example, how we have gone to extremes in sexual depravity and perversion, on the screen and on the stage. Nature has no other way than to cause us to swing back to the opposite. Nature always seeks a balance. When you misuse the law of your life, you may find yourself in a hospital cot. Perhaps you might call it a nervous breakdown, but it is benign nature compelling you to get back on the beam of harmony, and peace of mind.

We used to live under the old Victorian taboos and strictures; then came a violent swing to the opposite, the Freudian Era, with its emphasis on sex, followed by looseness, immorality and aberrations of all kinds. Change eternal is at the root of all things.

Every day you read about wars, eruptions, strife, ambushes, civil wars, bombings, kidnappings, etc. Ask yourself: What can I do about this? How can I retain my peace and sense of security in this changing world? You can feel secure and retain your peace, tranquility and serenity only by tuning in mentally with the Infinite Spirit, Which lies stretched in smiling repose. It is the Primal Cause.

Affirm boldly: "Divine love fills my soul. Divine peace saturates my mind and heart. The Light of God enfolds me, and I am inspired from On High." Turn your eyes to the hills, from which cometh your help, and the response will come.

You know how the masses think. They are always going from one extreme to the other extreme. There is war for a period, followed later by a period of peace. When these violent swings take place, many are hurt except those who tune in with the Infinite and who dwell in the Secret Place of the Most High.

Don't Be One of the Herd

Wherefore come out from among them, and be ye separate, saith the Lord, and touch not the unclean thing; and I will receive you, and will be a Father unto you, and ye shall be my sons and daughters, saith the Lord Almighty (II Corinthians 6:17-18).

In these wonderful verses you are told to come out from the mass mind and do your own thinking. You are told specifically not to touch the unclean thing, which means you are not to mentally dwell upon murder, hate or indulge in any form of negative thinking. On the contrary, you are to keep prayed up, which means that you constantly identify mentally and emotionally with the eternal verities of life, which are always the same yesterday, today and forever. As you keep prayed up, you won't suffer like the masses do.

The Law of Averages

The Law of Averages refers to the way the mass mind thinks. There are over four billion people in the world today, and they are all thinking into the one mind. It is safe to say that most of their thinking is very negative. There are, of course, a great number of spiritually oriented people who are thinking constructively, but they are in the minority.

The mass mind believes in sickness, disease, war, misfortune, crime, poverty, accidents, and calamities and catastrophes of all kinds. Moreover, millions of people are full of jealousy, hate, resentment, envy and hostility. These mental poisons bring on all manners of turmoil and conflict in the individual and collective lives of people. If you do not do your own spiritual thinking, the mass mind, called the Law of Averages, does your thinking for you.

True thinking is free from all fear, worry and negative activity of all kinds. We are all immersed in this mass mind, and we must establish counter convictions to all the false beliefs and destructive thoughts of the mass mind. If you were 100% vigilant in the sense that all your thoughts and imagery were based on spiritual principles and Divine truths, then you would be completely immune; but I doubt if anyone walks in that state of consciousness all the time. Therefore, undoubtedly, the negative mental atmosphere of the mass mind impinges on the subjective mind of all of us.

What Do You Believe?

Believe in the goodness of God in the land of the living. Believe in the guidance of the Infinite Presence and Power and the abundance and riches of the Infinite. Realize that God's riches—spiritual, mental and material—are forever circulating in your life, and that there is always a surplus. Believe in the Divine principles of harmony, right action, Divine law and order, and Divine love in the same way that a chemist believes in the principles of chemistry, which are dependable, enabling him to bring forth marvelous compounds which bless humanity in countless ways.

Fear Is Faith in the Wrong Thing

Recently the newspapers reported a fire in a night club, in which many people were trampled to death and others burned to death. It also mentioned there was no occasion for the panic, as there were sufficient exits to take care of all the people present. There were several, however, who remained quiet and calm, and they found their way out without being hurt.

Fear had seized the people, and fear is contagious. Fear was the cause of their deaths—not the fire. Those who turned to the Infinite Presence and Power within and called on It for protection and guidance remained at peace, and the way opened up in Divine order. Place your faith in God, and then . . . *no evil (shall) befall thee, neither shall any plague come nigh thy dwelling* (Psalm 91:10).

Your faith in God is a conviction of God's present and continuous care. Faith in God is the star that shines in the darkness, revealing the way you should go. Modern scientists do not work in the dark. They work in the light of faith . . . *In quietness and in confidence shall be your strength* . . . (Isaiah 30:15).

Disciplining Your Mind

Fill your mind with the eternal verities. Identify with the Spirit within you, knowing and believing that Divine love watches over you in all your ways. If you are careless, negligent, apathetic, listless and refuse to discipline your mind regularly, then you are subject to the influence of the mass mind; and you should not be surprised when reverses and sickness come. When the Asian flu is prevalent, you don't want to be one of the herd that takes what comes. By enthroning God-like ideas and spiritual values in your mind and filling your mind with constructive thinking, you will be invulnerable and immune to all harm; and you can't be sick, hurt or defeated.

Reading Your Mind

Recently during one of my seminars on the sea, I saw a woman read the minds of about ten of the passengers, all of whom were strangers to her. They agreed that she was about 90% accurate. This woman was a sensitive, a professional psychic. She tapped the subconscious of these passengers. Actually, what happened was that they told her everything before she told them anything. She got into a psychic, passive, receptive state of mind, a sort of semi-trance. In that state, she was able to read and sense the contents of their subconscious mind. She predicted marriage for some, travel for others to European countries, financial reverses for some, and a divorce for one member of the group.

There is nothing new in having the gift of extrasensory perception. Everyone possesses extrasensory perception, but these faculties may be dormant. Dr. J.B. Rhine of Duke University has conducted experiments for over thirty years and has revealed the capacity of clairvoyance, telepathy, clairaudience, telekinesis, retro-cognition and pre-cognition among students and others. His scientific findings have been acknowledged all over the world. His wife, Dr. Louisa Rhine, who is the author of *Hidden Channels of the Mind*, has revealed various forms of extrasensory perception in personal experience and recorded by men and women in all walks of life.

It is true that the future is in your mind now. The reason a clairvoyant can examine the contents of your mind is that the thought and the thing, or experience, are one in mind. Your mind is timeless and spaceless. For example, if you are contemplating a divorce, a good psychic or medium could tell you that you were planning a divorce, but it still does not have to happen objectively. You could change your mind and have a reconciliation. Nothing is foreordained or predestined. It is true that the divorce has taken place in your mind, but time moves slowly from the fourth dimension to this third-dimensional plane; therefore, it has not yet happened objectively.

Likewise, the reverses or illnesses predicted by a psychic, medium, clairvoyant or card reader, all of whom simply tap your subconscious mind, can be neutralized by scientific prayer, thereby preventing the negative experiences from occurring.

Scientific prayer means that you think from Universal Principles, such as: Divine law and order govern my life. Divine right action reigns supreme. Divine love saturates my soul. Divine peace fills my mind and heart. Divine guidance governs me in all ways. Divine harmony governs me, and all my ways are pleasantness and all my paths are peace.

As you change your mind by meditating on these truths, your whole world, body, circumstances and experiences will magically melt in the image and likeness of your contemplation. Your avoidance of the negative patterns that may be lodged in your subconscious mind will depend on your spiritual awareness and on the enlargement of your consciousness by scientific prayer. As you ascend spiritually, you will automatically avoid the negative experiences of the mass mind.

Leading a Balanced Life

You will notice in life that extremes always reverse themselves. When people go too far to any extreme, they are violently thrown back later to the other extreme. You are here to lead a balanced life, one of creativity, of peace, harmony and the joyous achievement of your purposes here. As you charge your mental and spiritual batteries regularly, you will neutralize the toxins of the mass mind to a great extent, and you won't suffer from the great swings of fate or the ups and downs of life. You will operate on an even keel, and the sicknesses, sorrows and tragedies of life will not be experienced by you.

If you allow your mind to be hypnotized or thought into by negative newscasters and prophets of doom and gloom, then these thoughts, as they become subjectified, will govern you negatively and destructively. Prayer is the contemplation of the truths of God from the highest standpoint, and you become what you contemplate.

The Good Seed

The Bible says: . . . *The kingdom of heaven is likened unto a man which sowed good seed in his field: But while men slept, his enemy came and sowed tares among the wheat, and went his way* (Matthew 13:24-25).

All of us are gardeners, and the good seeds represent the good thoughts we think all day long. The enemy is the negative suggestion, or the thoughts of the mass mind, which may be accepted by your mind if you are not on the *qui vive*, alert and quickened by the Holy Spirit. Negative thoughts and suggestions bombard us silently and audibly every day. The thing to do for maximum happiness is to continue saturating your mind with Divine ideas, and then there will be no room for the negative suggestions of others to enter.

Your subconscious mind responds to the convictions held by your conscious mind. You must really believe what you affirm; longing to believe is not enough. A woman who counseled with me recently said, "I keep affirming: God is all there is: the only Presence, Power, Cause and Substance." Nevertheless, at the same time she was full of fear of another woman who she said was practicing voodoo against her. Her words were pure verbalisms. She really did not believe what she affirmed.

I explained to her that the suggestions of others had no power to create the things they suggest and that she had the power to reject all negative suggestions. Actually, I explained that she was transferring the power within herself to the other woman, making her into a sort of a goddess with power to hurt her. The only Power is God. This Presence moves as unity, harmony, beauty and love. When your thoughts are God's thoughts, God's power is with your thoughts of good.

She began to understand that when you can't give hate, ill will, resentment or hostility you can't receive it. That's a simple observation. Therefore, if another person bombards you with negative thoughts and suggestions, you can't receive them and they return to the sender with double force, which is called the boomerang.

Judge Thomas Troward, author of *The Hidden Power*, states a magnificent truth on Page 134 of that book: "Once you admit that there is any power outside yourself, however beneficent you may conceive it to be, you have sown the seed which must sooner or later bear the fruit of 'fear,' which is the entire ruin of life, love and liberty. There is no via media." He emphasizes in his teaching that we are this Life-Principle Itself and that the difference is only that between the generic and the specific of the same thing.

This woman of whom I spoke, who was afraid of voodoo suggestions, used the following prayer regularly and, as a result, was completely freed from fear:

"God is all there is. One with God is a majority. *If God be for us who can be against us?* (Romans 8:31). I know and believe that God is the Living Spirit Almighty—the Ever-Living One, the All-Wise One— and there is no power to challenge God. I know and accept completely that when my thoughts are God's thoughts, God's power is with my thoughts of good. I know I cannot receive what I cannot give, and I give out thoughts of love, peace, light and goodwill to this person or persons (mention name or names) and to everyone else. I am immunized and God-intoxicated, and I am always surrounded by the sacred circle of God's love. The whole armor of God surrounds me and enfolds me. I am Divinely guided and directed, and I enter into the joy of living. *In thy presence is fullness of joy; at thy right hand there are pleasures for evermore* (Psalm 16:11)."

Seeing People in Their True Light

The way to look at people who say they are using voodoo, black magic, sorcery, etc., is to see them for what they really are. That is to say, they are men and women who are terribly ignorant of the real Spiritual Power. They imagine they have power, but they don't. To see and understand this is to cease to give any power to them.

The real and ultimate power is that of the affirmative. Their negative suggestions have no power except you accept the suggestions, which then become the movement of your own thought.

Your affirmation of Divine love, Divine harmony and Divine right action governing you destroys all negative suggestions and builds up life, health and happiness. The ultimate affirmative position is your conscious unity with Infinite Spirit within you—the Source of all Life. Realize your oneness with God and feel a genuine goodwill to all, and then you need not trouble about negative suggestions.

Why Do We Suffer?

We suffer because of our misapplication and misuse of universal laws and principles. As long as we deviate from the Golden Rule and the law of harmony we will suffer. It is correct to say that ignorance is the only sin and all the suffering in the world is the consequence. Our suffering causes us to seek the answer. In that way we awaken to the light within, and we discover our Divinity. We must use the law righteously. That means to think right, to feel right, to act right and to do right; then we will no longer suffer due to our ignorance of the laws of life and the way of the Spirit.

The So-Called Pious People

There are many so-called pious people who look down at those who don't believe the way they do. These *good* people blindly follow all the tenets, rules and regulations of their church. No doubt, they feel self-righteous and have, perhaps, a holier-than-thou attitude. Oftentimes they are full of condemnation and resentment toward those who don't conform to their superstitious and ignorant beliefs.

These negative attitudes bring on reverses, illnesses and neuroses. Many times when setbacks and tragedies come into their lives, they get angry at God and can't understand that religion is of the heart; not of the lips. Furthermore, they have forgotten the law that we become what we condemn. Religion means "to bind back." We should be bound to the Source of All life, to Divine love, Divine peace, Divine truth and Divine beauty. When these truths govern and dominate us, we will automatically express them, and the fruits of our religion will be made manifest.

Libertines and Profligates

Many devout and religious men at one time or another have engaged in drunken orgies and sexual excesses. St. Augustine once said, "Lord, grant me chastity," and then, as an afterthought, said, "Not yet." St. Francis led rather a wild life in his youth, and then in later life went to the other extreme when he practiced rigidities, austerities and mortification of the flesh. He went to extremes in his practice of penitential discipline, believing that this was the way to strengthen his will and overcome the negativity of his past.

At one time in his life, he realized his error and said, "Too late, I have beaten my brother." By his brother, he meant his body, which he mistreated. He forgot what Paul had said: . . . *Glorify God in your body* . . . (I Corinthians 6:20).

Remember, there is a reciprocal relationship between your thought and the Supreme Power within you. The power of suggestion is a hidden power, but the Power which creates all things is *the* Hidden Power, which is behind all creation and is one and indivisible. It moves only as harmony, wholeness, beauty and perfection. There is nothing to oppose the Infinite, challenge It, thwart or vitiate It. It is Omnipotent, Omniscient and Omnipresent. This is why it is written: . . . *If God be for us, who can be against us?* (Romans 8:31).

The Meaning of Israelite

In the symbolism of the Bible, an Israelite is any person who aligns with the Divine Spirit within, looking upon the Living Spirit Almighty as the only Presence, Power, Cause and Substance, and giving It complete allegiance. As you turn to It, there is a reciprocal response, and this power flows through you as harmony, health, peace, joy and prosperity. This is why it is written in Numbers 23:23: *Surely there is no enchantment against Jacob* (a man awakening to the Presence and Power of God), *neither is there any divination against Israel . . . But against any of the children of Israel shall not a dog move his tongue . . .* (Exodus 11:7).

15

The Top Secret

For the Lord thy God is a consuming fire . . . (Deuteronomy 4:24). *For thy Maker is thine husband* . . . (Isaiah 54:5).

I am writing this chapter at the Sands Hotel in Las Vegas, Nevada, where you meet people from every state of the Union. After concluding a session on the Secrets of the I Ching, a man from Georgia said to me, "Religion has failed. Look at the world today." Religion means to tie back—to relink yourself to the Source, which is God. If man mentally and spiritually tied himself to love, light, truth, beauty and joy, and if these truths dominated his mind, it would be a different world. That which binds you is your religion.

Fear dominates millions of people, a condition which leads to sickness, crime, frustration and anger. Superstition also binds and restricts millions of people. The dominant idea which governs and controls you could be called your religion. A man may call himself a Catholic, Protestant, Jew, New Thought, Hindu, Moslem, etc. All this means, however, is that he subscribes to what he was taught or what is preached to him. The real religion of every man is based on what he sincerely believes in his heart, such as his emotional espousals, his convictions, his deep-seated beliefs about life, God, the universe and himself. It is his subconscious drives, compulsions and conditioning that are made manifest in his life.

Man's subconscious assumptions, beliefs and convictions dictate and control all his conscious actions. Religion is of the heart; not of the lips. It is man's thinking in the heart that is expressed as form, function, experience and events. The heart in the Bible is your subjective mind, your emotional and feeling nature. A wonderful religion would be to have your mind controlled by a God of love and look upon the Infinite Presence and Power within you as your guide, your counselor, your boss and the Source of all blessings. Any movement of your mind based on fear, ignorance, superstition or an unknown power cannot bring enlightenment into your life; only more darkness and confusion.

Symbols of Mystery

We must no longer look upon communion with the Indwelling Presence as a mystery. It is foolish to keep on repeating old platitudes and shibboleths about God, angels, the Only Son, devils, salvation, sin, heaven, hell, etc. The ecclesiastical language of 1800 or 1900 years ago must be explained in everyday language so that a boy of seven or eight can comprehend.

God is the Life-Principle in man. Angels are Divine ideas, inspiration or intuitive flashes that come from your subliminal depths in response to your conscious mind's requests. Every man is a son, or expression of the Infinite Life Principle. Devil means God upside down, a perverted or ignorant use of the One Power. It means to misuse the Law of Life and could be called misunderstanding. Salvation means a solution to your problem; freedom from fear, sickness, lack and limitation. Sin means to miss the mark. You are actually sinning when you fail to lead a full and happy life. Heaven is the Infinite Intelligence in which we live, move and have our being. It also means your mind at peace. Hell means self-imposed restriction, bondage, limitation. Self- forgiveness is heaven; self-condemnation is hell.

The Top Secret

When you say "I AM," you are announcing the Presence of God within you, as explained in the third chapter of Exodus. "I AM" means Pure Being, Life, Awareness, Self-Originating Spirit, Unconditioned Consciousness. In other words, it is a secret to millions of people, because they don't know that when they say "I AM," they are proclaiming the Presence of God within them. It is called "Om" in India, and many chant the word "Om" as a mantra. It is important that you know the meaning of the word "Om" before using it. In Sanskrit, mantra means an instrument of thought.

The Proper Perspective

It is necessary to have a balanced viewpoint and to observe the correct relationship of your mind with events in your life. Out of your subconscious mind are born all the experiences of your life. Your subconscious is your immaterial world, the seat of emotion, and is the realm of cause. Whatever you impress on your subconscious mind, good or bad, is expressed on the screen of space.

When the Bible speaks of the manger, it is referring to your subconscious mind. If you have been conditioned negatively, you can begin now to fill your subconscious mind with life-giving patterns of harmony, love, peace, joy, right action and beauty, thereby cleansing all the negative patterns that may be lodged there based on early training, indoctrination and false theological concepts. You can align yourself at this moment with the Infinite ocean of life, love, truth and beauty and let these qualities of God flow through you in transcendental loveliness, transforming your whole being into harmony, health and peace.

The Solar Allegory

All the religions of the world have an astronomical origin and significance. The ancient mystics who were illumined and inspired, and also past masters of the art of psychology and the story of the soul, realized that terrestrial changes in the northern latitude coincided with astronomical changes and they pointed out that psychological changes also could take place in man as he awakened to the light of God within him.

The Birth, Death and Resurrection of the Sun

As you know, the sun crosses the equator on the 21st of March, called the ingress of Aries; and all the seeds frozen in the ground are resurrected due to the warmth and actinic rays of the sun. It is said that the desert rejoices and blossoms as the rose. All nature seems to be resurrected; and for this reason the sun was called the savior of the world because it resurrected and saved people from the ice, snow and limitations of winter and brought them into the dawn of a new day.

Yearly, the sun proceeds to rise to the highest point in the heavens, then it begins to descend; and on the 21st of September it reaches the zodiacal sign of Libra, where the days and nights are equal. Then it descends below the equator, where it is said to die. It is then pierced by Scorpio and gets the lance of Sagittarius.

Then, symbolically, it remains in the tomb of Capricorn, Aquarius and Pisces for three days or three months, all of which is symbolic.

Then comes the resurrection of the sun again on the 21st of March. This is the drama of the sun, called the birth, death and resurrection of the sun god.

Allegorized Types of the Sun

The names Hercules, Bacchus, Zoroaster, Mithra, Apollo, Chrishna and Vishnu were allegorized types of the sun. The ancient masters of allegory in their writings spoke of their birth, death and resurrection (i.e., birth, death and resurrection of the sun).

The distinguished Bible scholar, Robert Taylor, of St. John's College, Cambridge, England, author of *Diegesis*, in his exhaustive research, reveals that the birth of the god, Mithra, from the days of an infinitely remote antiquity, was represented to have taken place in a stable and was celebrated throughout the whole northern world at midnight, the 24th of December, the most celebrated of all the magian festivals.

The Constellation Virgo, which comes to the line of the horizon at midnight, the 24th of December, was said to preside over his nativity. Mithra (the sun) was born in the stable of Augias; that is, in the station of the celestial goat, or Capricorn. Every Christmas Eve, exactly at 12:00 midnight, the sign Virgo rises in the eastern horizon; so it was said the sun was born of a virgin at midnight. The sun, or Capricorn, on the 24th of December begins to rise and move northward. It gradually redeems the earth from the darkness of winter.

The Chronicles of Alexandria

The most ancient chronicles of Alexandria attest to the existence and universal prevalence of this belief in Egypt. For ages before Christianity, Egypt consecrated the pregnancy of a virgin and the nativity of her son, whom they annually presented in a cradle for the adoration of the people. When King Ptolemy (350 B.C.) demanded of the priests the significance of this religious ceremony, they told him it was a mystery taught by their forefathers. The Egyptian God was called Serapis, which, when broken down, is Zor-Ab-Is, or sun, father and fire, which means the sun is the father of fire. Marcus Aurelius said that the Bishops of Serapis were known and recognized under the title of Bishops of Christ. Zorabis, or Serapis, means the Presence of God in man. Our Bible says: . . . *Thy God is a consuming fire* . . . (Deuteronomy 4:24).

Legends of the Hindu God

You will find a similar story to that of Mithra, even in the most minute circumstances, constituting the basis of the legends of the Hindu God, Chrishna, which means Christ, or Sun, symbolic of the Presence of God in man. This story dates from about 1700 B.C. and is almost identical with that in the second chapter of Luke. The names Jesus and Christ were quoted by the great astronomer of Arabia, Alboazer, as the names which, following the most ancient traditions of the Persians, the Chaldeans, the Egyptians, and of Hermes and Aesculapius, had been given to the child, who in the most ancient projection of the signs of the zodiac was represented as the son of the virgin of the month of August. "That child," says Alboazer, "some nations call Jesus, but, in Greek, is called Christus."

All of these stories are dramatizing the role of the sun, portraying it as the savior of our world. As previously mentioned, the sun moves northward on the 24th of December. It gradually melts the ice and the snow in the northern latitudes, finally crossing the equator and giving birth to spring and new life. The sun is symbolic of the Presence of God, or Eternal Light within each one of us. As we become aware of the Indwelling Presence, we will begin to melt our fears, anxieties and frustrations in the sunshine of God's love.

The Birth of Jesus, the Man

Research scholars do not know the true date of the actual birth of Jesus, the man mentioned in our Bible. There was controversy about the date in ancient times as to whether He was born on the 24th of December at midnight, which was the great feast of Saturnalia in Rome, or whether He was born on the 21st of March, the ingress of Aries, the spring equinox, which was also celebrated in all northern latitudes. Finally, it was decided by a vote in one of the councils; and they decided on the feast of Saturnalia, which celebrated the birth of the sun or light in the sign of Capricorn in the northern hemisphere.

The Birth of God in You

When you become aware of the Divine Presence within you, it is called a babe; i.e., your awareness of this Primal Power, your new concept of God, results in a new man being formed in embryo in your own subjective depths. Your dreams, aspirations, ideals and goals which have been frozen within you are waiting for you to warm them with faith and confidence in the God Presence within you, which can bring them to pass in Divine order on the screen of space.

The Virgin Mary

The I AM within you is the Virgin Mary, which is capable of infinite conceptions of Itself without the aid of any man. The word virgin in the Bible means a pure mind, or mind dedicated to God. The word Mary conies from "mare," meaning the sea, all of which means the pure stream of consciousness. Maya, the name of the mother of Buddha, has the same meaning. The words Queen of Heaven, Star of the Sea, Isis, Queen Esther, etc., all mean the same thing—the I AM, or Presence of God in your subconscious depths.

God, or I AM, gives birth to the entire cosmos and all things contained therein and is the only Presence and Power. Actually, all the symbols of Christmas have to deal with the human heart, or your subconscious mind. The star spoken of represents the Infinite Intelligence within you, which guides and directs you and reveals to you the answer.

You can claim that God is guiding you and revealing to you the answer or solution to your problem. Accept the truth that the nature of Infinite Intelligence is to respond to you, and you will receive an answer without the aid of any man. You can boldly affirm, "I am whole, perfect, strong, loving, illumined, prosperous and inspired." As you continue to affirm these truths and feel and believe what you claim, without the help or cooperation of anyone, you will express what you feel to be true. Remember, whatever you attach to I AM, you become.

Pilgrimage of Man

The journey of every man should be to the inner realm of his own mind where the Divine Presence dwells, and there realize that he is a son, or expression of the Living God and heir to all of God's riches.

Begin to affirm now that you are a son of God and that you are illumined from On High. Continue to affirm it and believe it, and as you do, you will be wrapping that new concept of yourself in the swaddling bands of light and love and laying it in the manger of your own subconscious mind. Your subconscious accepts what is impressed upon it, and you will find your whole world magically melting in the image and likeness of your new concept of yourself.

While talking with a man here in the Sands Hotel in Las Vegas, he began to say, "I can't get a healing. My arthritis is getting worse. I have had shots of cortisone, vitamins, applied lotions and liniments, and the pain has increased." Unfortunately, he was enthroning the idea of incurability and the hopelessness of despair and wrapping that dead concept in the clothes of unbelief and then laying it in the manger, or tomb, or womb of his subconscious mind. The words tomb and womb are synonymous in Bible language.

This man realized what he was doing, and I found that he was full of resentment, hostility and suppressed rage toward relatives. This was the reason he was getting no results from the therapy he was receiving. I gave him a spiritual prescription, advising him also that he should cooperate with his doctor, blessing him at all times.

This was the spiritual prescription: "I fully and freely forgive all my relatives (mentioning their names), and I forgive myself for harboring negative thoughts about them. I loose them all and let them go, and I sincerely wish for all of them health, peace, joy and all the blessings of life. Whenever I meet any one of them in my mind, I will immediately affirm, 'I have released you. God be with you.' God's Healing Love saturates my whole being. God walks and talks in me. The miraculous healing power flows through me, and I give thanks for the healing taking place now."

As he continued to practice this spiritual therapy, he wrote me in Beverly Hills, telling me that a tremendous physical improvement had taken place and that he no longer uses a cane. As he continues, I know a complete healing will result. At my suggestion, he also imagines the doctor as congratulating him on his miraculous healing. He does this every night prior to sleep, and he knows that this disciplined imaginary act will gradually sink into his subconscious mind and come to pass in Divine order.

The Holy Land

The Holy Land (the mind at peace) is within you. By turning to God in prayer, meditation and mystic visioning, you can realize harmony, health, peace, abundance and security here and now. The story of religions, including Christianity, is somewhat of a sorry tale with its recital of the cruelty of the Dark Ages and the rabid, emotionally motivated Crusades for the recapture of a geographical holy land. According to some records, thousands of young people joined these pilgrimages only to wind up in the slave marts of Egypt.

From this absurd excursion, there followed a commercialization of supposedly "holy" relics—the wood from the cross of Jesus, the veil of Veronica, the holy Shroud, etc., with some members of the clergy waxing rich from lumber yard proceeds in the effort to keep up the supply of splinters from the so-called cross of Jesus. All this points to the innate tendency of the five-sense man's blind passion for material pilgrimages to geographical centers prominent in history and fable. He fails to see and realize that the holy land is truly within himself.

It takes a truly spiritual renaissance, a reawakening and rebirth to discover and become aware that "the birth of Jesus" is something much more than an historical event and is not to be found in a geographical location called Bethlehem. Man must awaken and realize that he is here to give birth to love, light, truth and beauty and can do so by meditating on these truths until they are absorbed into his mentality.

The Road to Bethlehem

The symbols of the child, the mother, the star, the manger, etc., antedate all known religions. They symbolize processes of spiritual awareness, rebirth and inner transformation. Prayer is the contemplation of the truths of God from the highest standpoint, and as you continue to dwell on the eternal verities, your whole personality will change. Your disposition and temperament will then become more God-like every day.

Bethlehem means the house of bread, which means that you meditate and focus your attention on the blessed bread of peace, joy, love, harmony and goodwill, for these are the real bread of God. Bethlehem is the City of David. The latter name means the beloved of God, a certain stage of awareness wherein you give all your allegiance and loyalty to the One Presence and Power. As you enthrone in your conscious mind God's ideas, you will generate a wonderful emotion, making your heart a chalice for His love; then wonders will begin to happen in your life. You must realize that the birth story of Jesus symbolizes the birth of God in you, and that all characters of the nativity represent your inner thoughts, moods, feelings, beliefs, urges and drives.

The Names in the Nativity

Joseph represents your conscious, reasoning mind with its superficial beliefs, opinions, creeds, dogmas, traditions, thoughts and fears—the five-sense man who judges according to appearances. Joseph also means imagination and the autocratic intellect.

Mary represents the subconscious mind, full of wisdom and intelligence, the seat of intuition, memory and emotion. Within your subconscious is the I AM, the Higher Self, sometimes referred to as the Superconscious. Mary is with child of the Holy Ghost (the Holy Spirit, the Presence of God), and Joseph is instructed to keep away, which means that your conscious mind is not to impregnate and browbeat your subconscious with its false sense-knowledge. Joseph is the guardian of the threshold and is to see to it that nothing enters into the subconscious that does not fill the soul with joy. Joseph (the conscious mind) should protect the subconscious from all pollution and negative impressions.

Jesus and Joshua are synonymous. Both names mean the same thing; i.e., God is your Savior, or God is the Emancipator. In other words, God within you is the solution to all your problems. The realization of your heart's desire is your savior. For example, if you are in prison, freedom is your savior; if sick, health is your savior; if dying of thirst, water would be your savior; and if lost in the jungle, God, or the Guiding Principle, would lead you out.

The inn is the outer meeting place of superficial human beliefs, fears, customs, traditional concepts, and beliefs of the mass mind. In other words, it is the law of averages, what the mass mind is thinking. When you inform the average man that the Infinite Intelligence within him can heal his body, inspire him, guide him and reveal to him all answers, and that It actually is the Presence of God, he all too frequently rejects it and instead postulates an anthropomorphic being up in the skies who judges, punishes and condemns. There is no room in his mind for the realization that his awareness of the Presence and Power of God and his contact and application of It in his life is his real savior.

The stable is the subconscious mind, the place where the "animi" or "animals" (basic urges, feelings, emotions, passions) are to be found waiting for the coming of the Shepherd, the Lord and Master. The Shepherd is your dominant conviction of God and the truths of life which keep a check on the sheep (the harmonious feelings and ideals) lest the wolves (destructive emotions) eat them up or destroy them. Your thoughts need a shepherd, which means your dominant idea of the goodness and love of God in the land of the living controls all lesser thoughts and emotions, actions and reactions.

The nativity, or birth of God, is taking place in you when you begin to radiate light, love, truth and beauty to all those around you and to all people everywhere. Become a channel for Divine love, harmony, peace and joy, and all the Divine forces will hasten to minister to your eternal growth and expansion in the light.

Santa Claus

The Christmas story and the Santa Claus of the ancients have points of psychological similarity and significance. Both point to the inner Reality in all of us. Children should never be disillusioned regarding the reality of Santa Claus, which one day will be translated into this Divine-Self awaiting recognition in life and life's purpose.

Mary is with child of the Holy Ghost, or Holy Spirit, or Presence of God, and needs no man for a husband. Isaiah says: *For thy Maker is thine husband* . . . (Isaiah 54:5). In other words, the five senses impregnate us with all kinds of sundry concepts, mostly negative, and we spawn an evil progeny when we permit ourselves to be governed by the five senses. We should enthrone God-like thoughts in our conscious mind; then we would have God as our husband.

The angel which announces to you the birth of God is your understanding and recognition that God indwells you and walks and talks in you. Claim, feel and know that you are now what you long to be, and without the aid of any man, you will conceive and bring to pass the new life, the new birth, the answered prayer.

Let Wonders Happen in Your Life

There is a mystic Power in you which can lift you up from the thralldom and bondage of sickness and make you whole, vital and bubbling over with enthusiasm. This Power can free you from the prison of fear and liberate you from all lack and limitation. It has a magical healing balm for the bruised heart. The God-Power can inspire you withnew thoughts and new ideas. It can reveal to you solutions for all your problems and lead you to your true place in life and reveal your hidden talents. It will bring new friends into your life and furnish you with prosperity that spells freedom to be, to do and to have. This Power is the Primal Power known to the ancient mystics for thousands of years. By contacting this Power through your thought and becoming an open channel for the influx of the Holy Spirit, you will soar up on wings like an eagle to the realm of dominion and joy.

Your conscious awareness of this Almighty Power and your determination to use It in your life is the birth of God in you called the child in the Bible. Nourish the idea that God indwells you and that His love fills your soul. As you contemplate and meditate on the truth that more and more of God is being expressed through you, wonders will happen in your life.

Your Morning Prayer

Begin every morning to affirm boldly: "God is guiding me now, and I predicate my success on the fact that the wisdom of God reveals to me everything I need to know. I am prospered and blessed beyond my fondest dreams. I am releasing more and more of wisdom, truth, love and beauty every day of my life, and I am always watched over by the Overshadowing Presence, which leads me to ways of pleasantness and paths of peace."

As you pray along the above lines, wonders will happen, and your whole life will be under the care of Divine wisdom.

Hear the Words of Isaiah

For unto us a child is born, unto us a son is given: and the government shall be upon his shoulder: and his name shall be called Wonderful, Counselor, The mighty God, The everlasting Father, The Prince of Peace (Isaiah 9:6).

This verse tells you that the government shall be on your shoulder, which means a government of Divine ideas, mothered by Divine love. This is the government of the free. This type of government enthroned in your own mind is the only government that will guarantee you peace, health, security, abundance and all the blessings of life.

Let God guide, direct and govern your life. Every day of your life affirm: "Divine love and order govern my life. Divine right action controls me. Divine love fills my soul. Divine success is mine now. Divine peace and harmony reign supreme in all phases of my life." As you continue to affirm these truths, they will sink down into your subconscious mind and come to pass. The government of your life will then be of God. Let the All-Wise One, the All-Knowing One, the Ever-Loving One, guide, heal and restore your soul.

God is the Great Counselor. If you are worried, perplexed or confused, e.g., if you do not know whether or not to take some important step, to accept a proposal, to sign a contract, to get a divorce, to accept a new position, to dissolve a partnership, to take a trip to Europe, or to proceed in a court action, claim that God puts the words into your mouth, and whatever you do, it is God doing it through you. The God-Presence will teach you new things utterly beyond the compass of your present understanding, enabling you to do what others think is impossible.

The Divine Government

As you make a habit of establishing the Divine government of God's ideas and eternal verities over your mind, body and activities, you will be guided, directed, and prospered along all lines. This new government of Divine law and order wipes away all tears and sets you on the high road to happiness, freedom and peace of mind. Christmas is the realization of the Power of God in you. It is your birthday in God.

16

The Bible and Woman's Bondage

From time to time in Bible classes, I am asked about certain passages of Paul, which seem confusing and perplexing to many women. One who intended to enter the Religious Science School of Ministry here in Los Angeles, which is open to all men and women who are interested and who meet the requirements, was told by her father that the Bible was opposed to women ministers.

He quoted the following verses from Corinthians: *Let your women keep silence in the churches: for it is not permitted unto them to speak; but they are commanded to be under obedience, as also saith the law. And if they will learn any thing, let them ask their husbands at home: for it is a shame for women to speak in the church* (I Corinthians 14:34-35).

This literal interpretation of the Bible has kept women in bondage for thousands of years. Her father was taking the Bible literally; but the Bible is a psychological and spiritual drama taking place in the consciousness of man. The Bible is not dealing with doctrinal questions or theological concepts, which are merely created by theologians out of their own mentalities.

The word *church* in the Bible does not refer to a building or a religious sect or denomination. Church means ecclesia, or a calling out or drawing forth of wisdom, truth and beauty from your subjective depths. It could be called an aggregation of spiritual ideas in your own mentality. To enter the church, or ecclesia, of God, you must adopt a new mental attitude and realize that God is Spirit and that you are one with that Spirit.

Many men have read the Bible in the letter, forgetting the spirit, or real inner meaning. Their different interpretations of the Scriptures, together with their promulgation of certain creeds and dogmas, are the main cause of the countless sectarian groups or churches of today. The writer would like to emphasize that the true church is within yourself and is not made of creeds, rituals, forms or ceremonies, nor is it contained in marble structures or those of wood and stone.

Your own heart (your subconscious mind) is the temple of the Living God, and the Spirit of Truth in you will guide you into all Truth. There is only One Truth—not two, three or 1000—just the One. Turn to the Spirit within, which is God, and ask for light and inspiration, and all the different creeds and dogmas will vanish. You will then find the true church within yourself—the Presence of God. Men and women in the Bible refer to the interaction of your conscious and subconscious mind. Woman means your subconscious mind, where the infinite intelligence and boundless wisdom of God abide. Emerson says, "The Infinite lies stretched in smiling repose." In other words, God lies in your subjective depths. When you pray for inspiration and guidance, or are seeking light on some subject, naturally you remain silent, still and receptive. As you know, the nature of Infinite Intelligence is responsiveness, and you use your conscious mind to carry out the guidance and inspiration which comes from it.

This procedure has nothing to do with sex or whether you are male or female. In other words, the Bible is not referring to sex but to gender. Everyone is male and female in the sense that every person has a conscious and a subconscious mind.

The Silent Treatment

When you pray for another you realize, as Paul says: *God is not the author of confusion, but of peace, as in all churches of the saints* (I Corinthians 14:33).

A saint, biblically speaking, is any person who is dedicated to God and the eternal principles of life. To pray scientifically for another person, you quiet the mind, remain still and passive. You don't try to make something come to pass. You seek results, but you don't try to coerce the subconscious to obey your decrees. Your subconscious responds to your convictions regarding the Infinite Healing Presence.

In the prayer process, you don't dwell on symptoms, aches or pains; neither do you say, "John (or May) is getting better now; his nerves are calmer, his heart is normal." These are suggestions but not a real silent realization. For example, if you are praying for Mary Jones, affirm: "Mary Jones is known in Divine Mind. God indwells her, and His river of peace saturates her mind. His love fills her soul. God is, and His Presence flows through her vitalizing, healing and restoring her to wholeness and perfection. I give thanks for the healing power of God taking place now."

In this prayer form, you identified with the Divine Presence in Mary, and you claimed that what is true of God is true of her. After your silent, spiritual treatment, if you felt an inner sense of peace or satisfaction or if you felt that is the best you could do for the present, dismiss the matter until you feel led to pray again. The next time you pray for her should be as if you had not prayed before. If, after the first time you prayed, you said, "This will do until I get back to it again," you would stultify your prayer. Each time you pray for Mary, you are reinforcing the idea of vitality and wholeness for her. Gradually, or immediately, as the case may be, the idea of perfect wholeness and vitality will be resurrected in Mary.

When you relax and let go and enter into a psychic, passive state, your conscious mind is partially submerged and you are *en rapport* subjectively with Mary; and what you feel as true of Mary will be felt by her. When you prayed, you were the silent one in your own church, knowing that God is the author of peace and health; not sickness or confusion. Your subconscious does not speak or articulate like your conscious mind. Your conscious mind dwells on wholeness, beauty and perfection and decrees joy and vitality. There is a response from the subconscious according to the beliefs and convictions of the conscious mind. That is why it is written: . . . *For it is not permitted unto them to speak* . . . (I Corinthians 14:34).

Your subconscious speaks in symbols, allegories, dreams and visions of the night. Your conscious mind may interpret and become the spokesman for your subconscious mind.

Ask Your Husband

For thy Maker is thine husband . . . (Isaiah 54:5). When, therefore, Paul says: *And if they will learn any thing, let them ask their husbands at home* . . . (I Corinthians 14:35), the answer is obvious. You are to turn to the Infinite Intelligence within you for guidance, right action, inspiration and direction. You are not to impregnate yourself with the negative thoughts, fears and false beliefs of the world, but, rather, enthrone God-like ideas and eternal verities in your conscious mind. As you busy your mind with these constructive thought patterns, your subconscious will respond accordingly. This applies to you regardless of your sex status.

Religious Restrictions on Women Are Based on Ignorance

After the above explanation to the woman at the opening of this chapter, she rejected completely the false interpretation given to the Bible by her father and decided to become a minister. Paul says: *Who also hath made us able ministers of the new testament; not of the letter, but of the spirit: for the letter killeth, but the spirit giveth life* (II Corinthians 3:6).

The Bible is now being taught from the standpoint of its spiritual or esoteric meaning, and women are gaining their freedom from the false and ignorant interpretations of the Scriptures.

The Veil

Another question I am frequently asked is why in many parts of the world, even today, women wear veils. This form of apparel is, of course, gradually dying out as more and more women are standing up for their rights, prerogatives and privileges. Men and women are equal in the eyes of God . . . *Male and female created he them* (Genesis 1:27).

The greatest degree of freedom for women is in our own country; and complete emancipation, spiritually, mentally, physically and financially, is already on the horizon. Woman represents the subjective side of life, which is invisible and covered by the objective side of life. The veil is symbolic of that truth.

Superstitions and Religion

It is sad but true that religion and superstition have been the prime offenders in advising people to belabor their bodies with all kinds of stern austerities for no good purpose. In ancient times many religious devotees practiced flagellations, privation and starvation, which were forms of mental and physical debauchery. Many of these religious devotees maltreated their bodies so much that they actually ruined them for the remainder of their lives. It is said that Saint Francis spent the last year of his life in a deep childish melancholy, "because," said he, "I brought this body to this pass. Because I have beaten my brother (his body) too hard."

The Biological Rule

It is true that down through the ages man in his ignorance has taken advantage of woman's biological handicap. She gave birth to children and devoted many years in bringing up the children to where they could be independent and support themselves. During all this time she has been under a physical handicap, and man has taken advantage of that for his own aggrandizement and to make her an inferior.

Many religions misread and misinterpreted the allegory of the Garden of Eden in order to justify keeping women in subjection . . . *And thy desire shall be to thy husband, and he shall rule over thee* (Genesis 3:16). It is stupid to take this literally. It is true psychologically, as previously explained. Your conscious mind rules your subconscious, and the latter is amenable and subservient to the suggestions of your conscious mind.

The Council of Alexandria

In the early days of Christianity, there was held a council of the church fathers in Alexandria. The purpose of this meeting was to decide whether women really possessed a soul or not. Lo and behold, they voted on the matter, and the conclusion was that she had—by a majority of one. I told this to my secretary, Mrs. Wright, and she said, "That was a close call."

We are now beginning to have women ministers in the Protestant churches, but since the early days of Phineas Parkhurst Quimby, 1847, onward, we have had women ministers in Unity, Religious Science, Science of Mind, Divine Science, Church of Truth, and all branches of the New Thought field. Recently, women priests have been ordained in the Episcopal Church, and it is only a question of time until we have women priests and bishops in the Catholic Church. It is also quite possible, at some time in the future, to have a woman pope.

The Middle Ages

There were many famous abbesses—superiors in a convent of nuns—in the Middle Ages who had their own establishments, who were illumined and inspired, and who became so outstandingly brilliant that they far outshone the men of that day. The men became frightened and nipped their distinguished and illustrious spiritual careers in the bud. These abbesses were distinguished scholars and outstanding executives also, and their male colleagues decided to clip their wings.

If these men had known the truth, they would have rejoiced and been exceedingly glad that members of their religious order had moved onward, upward and Godward. To inhibit and block another is to place blocks in your own progress and advancement.

Zoologists and naturalists inform us that there is no animal living under instinct dominating a female, though there are a few instances where the female dominates the male. Down through the ages man has dominated the female through the misuse of his mind, and he has exploited the female of the species because of her biological role in life.

Allegories Are Like Dreams

Allegories can be read at different levels like dreams. Many have more than one interpretation. Adam and Eve represent your conscious and subconscious mind. The serpent that tempts you represents your five senses, which deceive you and trick you at times. You must not be governed by your five senses, however, which consist of sundry concepts, good and bad. Five-sense knowledge is not sufficient to govern your life, for then you become impregnated with all sorts of false knowledge, fears, doubts and negative suggestions.

There are several levels to the Garden of Eden story, but actually, you are the Garden of Eden yourself. The four rivers represent your spiritual, mental, emotional and physical natures. They also represent an allegory of your body, representing the four fluid systems of your body: the cerebro-spinal nerve system, the sympathetic nerve system, the blood stream or circulatory system, and the intestinal tract.

The flora and fauna of the Garden, the plant and animal life, represent the flora and fauna of your body: the flora, the vegetation of the body; and the fauna, the cells of the body. This garden is tenanted by a man and woman—your conscious and subconscious mind. The allegory of the Garden of Eden is concerned with gender, not sex. It deals with the relationship of the male and female principle in all of us; namely, the conscious and subconscious mind.

Eve, the subconscious, was taken from Adam's rib while he slept. One way of looking at this is that during sleep the subconscious takes control and emerges. The rib-basket protects all the vital organs of your body. One meaning of the rib is the natural symbol of the preservative and protective nature of your subconscious. It is merely an allegory. During sleep, answers come in your dreams. Oftentimes the full solution to a perplexing problem is given to you then.

Years ago I used to see the questions to an examination in chemistry and pharmacology before the examination. Your subconscious controls all the vital processes while you sleep. The rib also means the structural idea or plan in your mind; and as you emotionalize the idea and become enthusiastic about it, you are calling forth Eve, the subjective or emotional, which is the creative medium. Emotion follows the thought, the idea, the invention in your mind. This is why in some countries in the Far East the woman follows the man. He goes first and she follows with a load on her head or back. He takes it easy.

This is the curse of literalism. It is said that a curse was pronounced upon Eve for listening to the serpent, and Eve was made subject to her husband. The subconscious is subject to the husband (conscious mind) not only for good, but for evil, too. It is foolish to listen to the serpent, which means, in simple language, the false beliefs of the world, five-sense propaganda.

The serpent is another name for the Life Principle, or God, only it means God upside down, a morbid, twisted, distorted concept of life, God and the universe. If you visit someone with cancer, are you bothered by the thought that you may get it? Where is the tempter? In your own mind. Slay the negative thought. Cremate it at once, and affirm: "Spirit in me is God. It is the Ever-Living One, the All Wise One. It can't be hurt. It is Omnipotent." This attitude will protect you.

The Two Trees

An allegory is a representation of the spiritual meaning through concrete or material forms. It is a figurative treatment of one subject under the guise of another. When I was a boy I asked the priest at my church where the Garden of Eden was. He said it was between the Tigris and the Euphrates and to ask no more questions. If a thing is true, there is a way in which it is true. There is no such garden any place and there never was an actual Garden of Eden.

But it is true psychologically. All of us have received instructions and ideas, both good and bad, false and true, when we were young and impressionable; and our minds, being malleable, accepted them. Like seeds, these ideas grew up in us and became fixed states of mind. Perhaps some were based on fear and prejudices and others on the golden rule, honesty, integrity, etc. Our religious beliefs were given to us when young and, like fruit on a tree, we bear fruit according to the beliefs implanted in our subconscious mind.

The religious wars of today bear bad fruit from the tree of life within ourselves. All seeds grow after their kind. The tree of good and evil is our own mind believing in good and evil, which is the cause of the troubles of the world. There is only One Power—not two, three or a thousand.

Old Customs and Traditions Based on Ignorance

Recently I conducted a class on the Inner Meaning of the Book of Romans, which was very well received. A young medical doctor who was present said she would appreciate the psychological and spiritual meaning of the following verses from Paul, which troubled her:

Every man praying or prophesying, having his head covered, dishonoureth his head. But every woman that prayeth or prophesieth with her head uncovered dishonoureth her head: for that is even all one as if she were shaven. For if the woman be not covered, let her also be shorn: but if it be a shame for a woman to be shorn or shaven, let her be covered. For a man indeed ought not to cover his head, forasmuch as he is the image and glory of God; but the woman is the glory of the man. For the man is not of the woman; but the woman of the man. Neither was the man created for the woman; but the woman for the man. For this cause ought the woman to have power on her head because of the angels (I Corinthians 11:4-10).

These verses of Paul deal with the interaction of the male and female principle within all of us. When these two phases of our mind work harmoniously, peacefully and in unison and accord, the issue from this union results in health, wealth, happiness and true expression.

There are some churches in Europe and South America as well as other places that still insist today that women cover their heads before entering the cathedral; however, the custom is dying out to a great extent. Some years ago a group of us visited some of the famous cathedrals in Italy and France. Some women from America had to put something on their heads in order to enter, and it wasn't always a hat. This is an old custom or tradition handed down for generations.

The marriage in the Bible is the union of your thought and emotion. When these two unite and are constructive, there is an issue from this union. If your thoughts are God-like, your emotions, being generated from your thought, your heart will then be a chalice of God's love. The real marriage in the Bible is your sense of oneness with God. From that union come forth all the fruits of God: love, joy, peace, abundance, security and happiness.

Paul is speaking about the subjective side of our nature, which is called woman in the Bible. A man or a woman is not to be looked upon just as a body. You are a mental and spiritual being. Your body is a vehicle and is a representation of your thoughts, feelings, imaginations and beliefs. Spirit, Consciousness, Awareness, the Life-Principle is the reality of each person.

Paul is always talking about spiritual laws and truths of life. Paul knew the workings of the mind and was well acquainted with what we call abnormal psychology today. For about 300 years the teachers and leaders of early Christianity performed great things, including miraculous healings, and were on fire with the Truth.

All of you know the history of the great Roman emperor Constantine, who came along and organized the early church into a vast organization, establishing rites, rituals, ceremonies, and doctrinal regulations, dogmas and tenets to be believed in. It grew on the outside but began to die slowly on the inside. This is true of all the religions. These men forgot the real Source of all blessings and bounty and looked to form, ceremony, structures and the hierarchy, worshipping the created thing rather than the Creator. Always look to your own Divine Center for the light and true wisdom.

When Verse 4 says: Every man praying or prophesying, having his head covered, dishonoured his head, man means mind—your conscious, reasoning mind, your thought, intellect. Your thought is incipient action. Man's head should be uncovered in the sense that his imagination should be disciplined and controlled along spiritual lines. His mind should be free from fear, arrogance, pride and strife. Spiritual reasoning should be enthroned, and thoughts of peace, harmony, right action and goodwill should dominate his conscious mind.

Paul says a woman should have her head covered, for he says it is a shame for a woman's hair to be shorn or shaved; let her be covered. We are told that Samson's strength was in his hair.

Hair represents thoughts and emanations of Divine energy, your mental patterns and attitudes. This is why man's hair is cut short. This should not be taken literally, as it has nothing to do with actual physical hair on the top of your head. Man trims or cuts off his hair, meaning he gets rid of all resentment, antagonism, prejudices and hostility. By identifying with Divine love, the Spirit of forgiveness and exalting God in the midst of him, then his head, or conscious mind, is truly uncovered and he is ready for prayer, meditation and spiritual growth. Looking at it symbolically and from a spiritual standpoint, long hair on a man would indicate a growth of false concepts and erroneous opinions accompanied by negative emotions, and intellectual pride and conceit.

Mrs. Margaret Barrows, who does some extra work for me occasionally, asked me why it was that women through the ages were looked upon as chattels, inferior to man, and subservient. She mentioned, for example, that one of her female antecedents in the old country in Europe would leave the room whenever a man came to visit her husband.

As previously explained, the subconscious is subservient to the conscious mind, or the man. The male (conscious mind, intellect) is dominant. This is why the woman, when she prays, should have a cover. All that means is that your conscious mind should be the guardian at the threshold and should see to it that nothing enters into your subconscious mind that does not fill your soul with joy.

If you see a builder laying bricks and one brick is underneath the other, both bricks are the same and of equal importance. The brick underneath is in an inferior position, not, however, inferior in usefulness and importance. One brick is inferior in placement or position, and that is all. This is the same with your subconscious, called the woman in the Bible. Your conscious mind controls and dominates your subconscious, and the latter is amenable to suggestions and the habitual thinking and imagery of your conscious mind.

Your subconscious responds to the dominant thought of your conscious mind. When your thought or idea is emotionalized, it is subjectified. Your subconscious, being creative, then causes the manifestation to take place. *Which of you by taking thought can add one cubit unto his stature?* (Matthew 6:27). To cubit in the Bible means to mother it, to emotionalize your idea, to nourish it and animate it so that it will gel and become impressed in the subconscious and come to pass.

The Woman in Everyone

One of our radio listeners, who has a secretarial position with the Government and is about to retire shortly, wrote me and said she heard me say on my daily radio broadcast that if you pictured yourself on board a plane or ship and felt the reality of it (for example, if you want a voyage on a ship, you should picture the event here and now, and feel yourself as now sitting on deck, looking at the stars, listening to the creaking of the ship, smelling the briny ocean, feeling the ocean breeze in your face and looking at the vast deep), by dwelling on the scene and making it so vivid and real that when you opened your eyes after the meditation period you are actually amazed that you are not on the ship. Your feeling was so real, that it is a sure sign that you have fixed it in your subconscious and it will come to pass. Even though you do not have the money to take the trip, if you succeed in impregnating your subconscious, it will surely come to pass in ways you know not of.

Accordingly, she followed the technique and on the third night fell asleep affirming, "Trip, trip, trip." She awakened the next morning and had no further desire to pray about it, because she had succeeded in fixing the idea in her subconscious mind. The sequel was interesting. She is retiring in a few months, and her supervisor proposed marriage. The first thing he said to her was: "After the marriage we are taking a trip around the world." Her prayer was answered and she is taking the trip that she had imagined and felt to be true.

This is what the Bible means by cubing your thought or mental image—mother it, for it is the mother that gives birth to the child—not the man. She began to think about the trip, got maps of foreign countries, and then, getting interested in visiting all the foreign ports, she engaged the powers of her subjective mind, because she evoked the feeling, the interest, the enthusiasm; then the subjective mind brought it to pass in its own way. The woman in you always represents your emotion, your feeling nature, your subjectivity.

Why the Woman's Head Must Be Covered

Your subconscious mind does not choose your thoughts. Your conscious mind is the choosing, volitional mind. This is why the subconscious mind can be polluted by an ignorant, tyrannical, despotic, egotistic and autocratic conscious mind. When the conscious mind entertains gangsters, assassins and marauders in the form of evil, hostile, hateful and vengeful thoughts, these befoul the subconscious and bring forth all manner of diseases and disorders of mind, body and affairs.

This type of conscious mind can be in every person, irrespective and regardless of sex. To indulge in resentment, or to desire to get even causes your subconscious to respond in a negative and destructive manner. Modern research by psychosomatic physicians points out that they have found destructive emotions behind cancer cases.

Mind Over Cancer

In an article on prevention in the *Magazine for Better Health*, Dr. Carl Simonton, a specialist in oncology, the science of tumors, states as follows: "Some personality characteristics of the cancer patient that other scientists have identified as significantly different than non-cancer patients are: (1) a tendency to harbor resentment and an impairment in his ability to express hostility; (2) a tendency towards self-pity; (3) difficulty in developing and maintaining meaningful, long-term relationships; and (4) a poor self-image. In addition, a sense of basic rejection, either by one or both of his parents, consequently develops the life history pattern seen so commonly in the cancer patient."

Dr. Simonton points out in the above quotation from his article that negative, destructive emotions can bring about destructive diseases in the human body. This is why the Bible says the woman's head (your subconscious) should be governed by Divine ideas, mothered by Divine love. This is the government of the free and it guarantees peace, security, health and abundance.

The Woman Is the Glory of Man

Verse 7 of Chapter 11 of I Corinthians is, of course, psychological. The woman (your subconscious) should always be watched over and protected by your conscious mind. The word glory comes from glow-ray; i.e., whatever thoughts are true, lovely, noble and God-like, when focused on by your conscious mind, will find their way by a process of spiritual osmosis, into your subconscious and shed their glow, warmth and light on all your undertakings.

If you do not govern, control and direct your emotional life, you will respond to all the sundry negative thoughts, fears and predictions of gloom and doom which bombard us night and day; then these irrational emotions will impel and propel you into negative actions and reactions. In Biblical language, you are committing adultery when you cohabit with evil, hate, jealousy, resentment and hostility in the bed of your mind. To do so is to spawn an evil progeny.

The woman's hair is not shorn or shaven, because hair, being symbolic of thought, should be protected at all times by the Truths of God and watched over by the Overshadowing Presence of a God of Love, enthroned and dominant in the conscious mind.

Man's hair, symbolically speaking, should be shorn, as previously explained, in the sense that his intellect should be anointed with the wisdom of God; and his contemplation should be on the truths of God from the highest standpoint. Down through the ages men have worn hair long and short, but the Bible is talking about your thought life, your mental patterns and focused attention. Long hair, symbolically and Biblically speaking, would be wrong for a man, as it would indicate that he was governed not by spiritual reasoning, but by negative emotions and the mass mind.

Woman's hair, Paul says, should not be shorn, which, in the psychological and spiritual sense, means that her mind is not at peace and that she does not have God or God-like thoughts or ideas, as her husband. In other words, ignorance, fear and superstition are governing her, and she is not clothed with the garment of salvation and the robe of righteousness. The woman who is uncovered, therefore, in the light of the Bible and its inner meaning, becomes unstable, neurotic and subject to every wind that blows.

Needless to say, whichever you are, a man or a woman, you do not take the subject of the hair literally. A man with long or short hair may be a God-like man. The trouble is not in his hair or head, but the way in which he uses the laws of mind. The answer to all problems is to keep your attention on God and all things good; then you are prophesying for yourself a wonderful future. With your eyes stayed on God, there is no evil on your pathway.

Disciplining the Mind

She was found with child of the Holy Ghost (Matthew 1:18).

The Holy Ghost means the Holy (whole) Spirit or God which is lodged in the unconscious depths of all men. Joseph is your choosing, volitional, or conscious mind. Mary represents your deeper mind full of the qualities, attributes, and potencies of God.

Joseph, the conscious mind, should be a guide and protector for the holy child, which child is your awareness of the presence and power of God within you. Your thought is Joseph, and your feeling or emotion is Mary. When these two unite in peace and harmony, your prayer is answered; this is God in action. This is the way your mind works, and knowledge of this is the birth of the Holy Child or wisdom in you.

Practice a harmonious, synchronous and joyous relationship between your conscious and subconscious mind and you will bring forth health, peace, strength and security. Enthrone the right idea in your mind; then you will experience in your heart the true feeling. The union of your thought and feeling represents the married pair in you; when they are fused, the third element, peace (God), enters in, and you experience the joy of the answered prayer. Let your heart become a chalice for God's love and a manger for His birth; as a result you will express and bring forth a child which is God on earth.

About the Author

Dr. Joseph Murphy was born on May 20, 1898, in a small town in the County of Cork, Ireland. His father, Denis Murphy, was a deacon and professor at the National School of Ireland, a Jesuit facility. His mother, Ellen, née Connelly, was a housewife, who later gave birth to another son, John, and a daughter, Catherine.

Joseph was brought up in a strict Catholic household. His father was quite devout and, indeed, was one of the few lay professors who taught Jesuit seminarians. He had a broad knowledge of many subjects and developed in his son the desire to study and learn.

Ireland at that time was suffering from one of its many economic depressions, and many families were starving. Although Denis Murphy was steadily employed, his income was barely enough to sustain the family.

Young Joseph was enrolled in the National School and was a brilliant student. He was encouraged to study for the priesthood and was accepted as a Jesuit seminarian. However, by the time he reached his late teen years, he began to question the Catholic orthodoxy of the Jesuits, and he withdrew from the seminary. Since his goal was to explore new ideas and gain new experiences—a goal he could not pursue in Catholic-dominated Ireland—he left his family to go to America.

He arrived at the Ellis Island Immigration Center with only $5 in his pocket. His first project was to find a place to live. He was fortunate to locate a rooming house where he shared a room with a pharmacist who worked in local drugstore.

Joseph's knowledge of English was minimal, as Gaelic was spoken both in his home and at school, so like most Irish immigrants, Joseph worked as a day laborer, earning enough to keep fed and housed.

He and his roommate became good friends, and when a job opened up at the drugstore where his friend worked, he was hired to be an assistant to the pharmacist. He immediately enrolled in a school to study pharmacy. With his keen mind and desire to learn, it didn't take long before Joseph passed the qualification exams and became a full-fledged pharmacist. He now made enough money to rent his own apartment. After a few years, he purchased the drugstore, and for the next few years ran a successful business.

When the United States entered World War II, Joseph enlisted in the Army and was assigned to work as a pharmacist in the medical unit of the 88th Infantry Division. At that time, he renewed his interest in religion and began to read extensively about various religious beliefs. After his discharge from the Army, he chose not to return to his career in pharmacy. He traveled extensively, taking courses in several universities both in the United States and abroad.

From his studies, Joseph became enraptured by the various Asian religions and went to India to learn about them in depth. He studied all of the major religions from the time of their beginning. He extended these studies to the great philosophers from ancient times until the present.

Although he studied with some of the most intelligent and far-sighted professors, the one person who most influenced Joseph was Dr. Thomas Troward, who was a judge as well as a philosopher, doctor, and professor. Judge Troward became Joseph's mentor. From him he not only learned philosophy, theology, and law, but also was introduced to mysticism and particularly, the Masonic order. He became an active member of this order and over the years rose in the Masonic ranks to the 32nd degree in the Scottish Rite.

Upon his return to the United States, Joseph chose to become a minister and bring his broad knowledge to the public. As his concept of Christianity was not traditional and indeed ran counter to most of the Christian denominations, he founded his own church in Los Angeles. He attracted a small number of congregants, but it did not take long for his message of optimism and hope rather than the "sin and damnation" sermons of so many ministers to attract many men and women to his church.

Dr. Joseph Murphy was a proponent of the New Thought movement. This movement was developed in the late 19th and early 20th centuries by many philosophers and deep thinkers who studied this phenomenon and preached, wrote, and practiced a new way of looking at life. By combining a metaphysical, spiritual, and pragmatic approach to the way we think and live, they uncovered the secret of attaining what we truly desire.

The proponents of the New Thought movement preached a new idea of life that brings out new methods and more perfected results, and we have the power to use it to enrich our lives. We can do all these things only as we have found the law and worked out the understanding of the law, which God seemed to have written in riddles in the past.

Of course, Dr. Murphy wasn't the only minister to preach this positive message. Several churches, whose ministers and congregants were influenced by the New Thought movement, were founded and developed in the decades following World War II. The Church of Religious Science, the Unity Church, and similar places of worship preach philosophies similar to this. Dr. Murphy named his organization The Church of Divine Science. He often shared platforms, conducted joint programs with his similar-thinking colleagues, and trained other men and women to join their ministry.

Over the years, other churches joined with him in developing an organization called the Federation of Divine Science, which acts an umbrella for all Divine Science churches. Each of the Divine Science church leaders continues to push for more education, and Dr. Murphy was one of the leaders to support the creation of the Divine Science School in St. Louis, Missouri, to train new ministers and provide ongoing educational education for both ministers and congregants.

The annual meeting of the Divine Science ministers was a must to attend, and Dr. Murphy was a featured speaker at them. He encouraged the participants to study and continue to learn, particularly about the importance of the subconscious mind.

Over the next few years, Murphy's local Church of Divine Science grew so large that his building was too small to hold them. He rented The Wilshire Ebell Theater, a former movie theater. His services were so well attended that even this venue could not always accommodate all who wished to attend. Classes conducted by Dr. Murphy and his staff supplemented his Sunday services that were attended by 1,300 to 1,500 people. These were supplemented by seminars and lectures that were held most days and evenings. The church remained at the Wilshire Ebell Theater in Los Angeles until 1976, when it moved to a new location in Laguna Hills, California, near a retirement community.

To reach the vast numbers of people who wanted to hear his message, Dr. Murphy created a weekly radio talk show, which eventually reached an audience of over a million listeners.

Many of his followers wanted more than just summaries and suggested that he tape his lectures and radio programs. He was at first reluctant to do so, but agreed to experiment. His radio programs were recorded on extra-large 78rpm discs, a common practice at that time. He had six cassettes made from one of these discs and placed them on the information table in the lobby of the Wilshire Ebell Theater. They sold out the first hour. This started a new venture. His tapes of his lecture explaining biblical texts, and providing meditations and prayers for his listeners were not only sold in his church, but in other churches, bookstores, and via the mail.

As the church grew, Dr. Murphy added a staff of professional and administrative personnel to assist him in the many programs in which he was involved and in researching and preparing his first books. One of the most effective members of his staff was his administrative secretary, Dr. Jean Wright. The working relationship developed into a romance, and they were married—a lifelong partnership that enriched both of their lives.

At this time (the 1950s), there were very few major publishers of spiritually inspired material. The Murphy's located some small publishers in the Los Angeles area, and with them produced a series of small books (often 30 to 50 pages printed in pamphlet form) that were sold, mostly in churches, from $1.50 to $3.00 per book. When the orders for these books increased to the point where they required second and third printings, major publishers recognized that there was a market for such books and added them to their catalogs.

Dr. Murphy became well known outside of the Los Angeles area as a result of his books, tapes, and radio broadcasts and was invited to lecture all over the country. He did not limit his lectures to religious matters, but spoke on the historical values of life, the art of wholesome living, and on the teachings of great philosophers—both from the Western and Oriental cultures.

As Dr. Murphy never learned to drive, he had to arrange for somebody to drive him to the various places where he was invited to lecture and other places in his very busy schedule. One of Jean's functions as his administrative secretary and later as his wife was to plan his assignments, arrange for trains or flights, airport pickups, hotel accommodations, and all the other details of the trips.

The Murphy's traveled frequently to many countries around the world. One of his favorite working vacations was to hold seminars on cruise ships. These trips were for a week or more and would take him to many countries around the world.

One of Dr. Murphy's most rewarding activities was speaking to the inmates at many prisons. Many ex-convicts wrote him over the years, telling him how his words had truly turned their lives around and inspired them to live spiritual and meaningful lives.

He toured the United States and many countries in Europe and Asia. In his lectures, he emphasized the importance of understanding the power of the subconscious mind and the life principles based on belief in the one God, the "I AM."

Dr. Murphy's pamphlet-sized books were so popular that he began to expand them into more detailed and longer works. His wife gave us some insight into his manner and method of writing. She reported that he wrote his manuscripts on a tablet and pressed so hard on his pencil or pen that you could read the page by the imprint on the next page. He seemed to be in a trance while writing. His writing style was to remain in his office for four to six hours without disturbance until he stopped and said that was enough for the day. Each day was the same. He never went back into the office again until the next morning to finish what he'd started. He took no food or drink while he was working, He was just alone with his thoughts and his huge library of books, to which he referred from time to time. His wife sheltered him from visitors and calls and kept things moving for church business and other activities.

Dr. Murphy was always looking for a simple way to discuss the issues and to elaborate points that would explain in detail how it affects the individual. He chose some of his lectures to present on cassettes, records, or CDs, as the technologies developed and new methods entered the audio field.

His entire work of CDs and cassettes are tools that can be used for most problems that individuals encounter in life, and have been time-tested to accomplish the goals as intended. His basic theme is that the solution to problems lies within oneself. Outside elements cannot change one's thinking. That is, your mind is your own. To live a better life, it's your mind not outside circumstances that you must change. You create your own destiny. The power of change is in your mind, and by using the power of your subconscious mind, you can make those changes for the better.

Dr. Murphy wrote more than 30 books. His most famous work, *The Power of Your Subconscious Mind*, which was first published in 1963, became an immediate bestseller. It was acclaimed as one of the best self-help guides ever written. Millions of copies have been sold and continue to be sold all over the world.

Among some of his other bestselling books were *Telepsychics—The Magic Power of Perfect Living, The Amazing Laws of Cosmic Mind,*

Secrets of the I Ching, The Miracle of Mind Dynamics, Your Infinite Power to Be Rich, and *The Cosmic Power Within You.*

Dr. Murphy died in December 1981, and his wife, Dr. Jean Murphy, continued his ministry after his death. In a lecture she gave in 1986, quoting her late husband, she reiterated his philosophy:

> I want to teach men and women of their Divine Origin, and the powers regnant within them. I want to inform that this power is within and that they are their own saviors and capable of achieving their own salvation. This is the message of the Bible and nine-tenths of our confusion today is due to wrongful, literal interpretation of the life-transforming truths offered in it.
>
> I want to reach the majority, the man on the street, the woman overburdened with duty and suppression of her talents and abilities. I want to help others at every stage or level of consciousness to learn of the wonders within.

She said of her husband: "He was a practical mystic, possessed by the intellect of a scholar, the mind of a successful executive, the heart of the poet." His message summed up was: "You are the king, the ruler of your world for you are one with God."